THE MIRROR
OF THE SKY

Hemanta Bāul (with dotārā) *in annual Bāul fair at Kenduli.*

THE MIRROR OF THE SKY

Songs of the Bāuls of Bengal

Translated from the original Bengali
with Introduction and Notes by

Deben Bhattacharya

Revised, Expanded Edition

HOHM PRESS
Prescott, Arizona

First published by George Allen & Unwin Ltd., Londo ι,
1969 for UNESCO Collection of Representative Works,
Indian Series; and as *Songs of the Bards of Bengal*, Grove
Press, New York, 1969.

Cover Design: Kim Johansen
Interior Design: Jaye Pratt, Alpha-Cat Design

Library of Congress Cataloging-in-Publication Data

The mirror of the sky: songs of the Baul's of Bengal /
    translated from the original Bengali with introduction
    and notes by Deben Bhattacharya. -- Rev. expanded ed.
    p.   cm.
    ISBN: 0-934252-89-0
    1. Bengali poetry--Translations into English. 2. Bauls-
    -India--West Bengal--Poetry. I. Bhattacharya. Deben.
PK 1771.E3M5 199   98-45834
891-4'41008--DC21   CIP

HOHM PRESS
P.O. Box 2501
Prescott, AZ 86302
800-381-2700
http://www.hohmpress.com

Manufactured in the United States of America

My life is a little oil lamp
floating on the waves.
But from which landing-pier
did you set me afloat?
With darkness ahead of me
and darkness behind,
darkness overlaps my night,
while the necklace of waves
constantly rings me about.
The storm of the night
relentlessly flows
below the stars,
and the lamp is afloat
on the shoreless water—
for company.

~ *Gangārām*

ACKNOWLEDGMENTS

I am deeply indebted to Christopher Nash for
generous guidance during my revising of the
manuscripts and for offering many valuable
suggestions. I must also express my gratitude to
Richard Lannoy, who read through the text and
gave me helpful advice concerning the introduction
while supplying me with some rare photographs
reproduced in this book, as indicated in the list of
illustrations. Furthermore, I am especially grateful
to Margot Moffett for her tireless assistance
through all stages in the preparation of the book.
Finally, my sincere thanks are due to Danica
Radman, a great lover of Oriental music and a
remarkable musicologist, who very kindly helped
me by writing the notation of the Bāul song which
is reproduced in the book.

CONTENTS

୶

ILLUSTRATIONS

Frontispiece   Hemanta Bāul (with *dotārā*) in
annual Bāul fair at Kenduli. *Photo:*
Deben Bhattacharya, 1973.

Page xviii   Nabanidās Bāul with Purna and
Sudhā in Calcutta. *Photo: Richard*
Lannoy, 1954.

Page xxiii   Nabanidās Bāul (with *aektārā*) in
Siuri. *Photo: Richard Lannoy, 1954.*

Page xxv   Purnadās Bāul (with the frame-drum
khañjari and the kettle-drum *duggi*)
during his tour of France. *Photo:*
Dominique Alisé, Espedaillac, 1990.

Page xxix   Nabanidās Bāul, in meditation.
Photo: Richard Lannoy, Suiri, 1954.

Page 27   Bāul instruments. *Photo: Richard*
Lannoy, Siuri, 1954.

Nabanidās Bāul with Purna and Sudhā in Calcutta.

PREFACE

❦

Born and brought up in a Bengali family of
Sanskrit scholars in Varanasi, I had the privilege
and the rare chance of being closely associated
with many great singers of religious songs. They
ranged from professional artists of the Raga music
to the itinerant Bāul singers from Bengali villages,
who often visited Varanasi to sing their songs of
faith and philosophy, expressing themselves in
words such as these:

He talks to me
but he would not let me see him.
He moves
close to my hands
but away from my reach.
I explore
the sky and the earth
searching for him, circling round my error of
not knowing my self.
Who am I
and who is he?

❧ Lālan[1]

In the lyrics of the Bāul, God is as illusive as the beloved, but attainable only through the knowledge of one's Self. His search, therefore, is not only for the Absolute, but also for the *Moner-Mānush*, or "the Man of the Heart," "the Man within."

To most Bengalis, the songs of the Bāuls represent an important part of the musical landscape of Bengal. When these songs are sung at home or out in the open air, the audience and the artists often consist of both Hindus and Muslims, unlike in their respective places of worship where only the adherents of the religion participate in the formal prayers and hymns. There, as the Bāul regrets:

Doors of love bear many locks—
Scriptures and beads.

✍ Madan

The word Bāul, as traceable for the first time in written literature, appears in the fifteenth-sixteenth century Bengali poetic works, *Shri Krishna-vijaya* by Maladhar Basu and *Chaitanya-charitāmrita* by Krishnadas Kaviraj. It is generally

---

[1](from previous page) Most song composers are identified in the Biographical Notes, p. 206.

agreed that the word Bāul in Bengali is a derivation
of Sanskrit *Vātula,* meaning insane, affected by the
wind. Lovingly said, the Bāul is God's vagabond.
And the expression "God's vagabond" could
easily be applied to Nabanidās Bāul, whom I heard
singing at an open-air gathering in Calcutta, accom-
panied by his son Purna Dās—who was nineteen at
the time—and a young disciple named Sudhā Bāul.
True to the Bāul's description of himself,
Nabanidās was "wholly dedicated to his own
nature. He laughed or cried, danced or sang as he
wished" in front of nearly a thousand-strong
spellbound audience. During a music conference
organized by young intellectuals of the city in a
public park at the center of Calcutta, Nabanidās
addressed his listeners from a raised platform,
erected at one end of the park:

Ōhé guni, ko-ōnā shuni,
tumi kōn guné mānush hō-échhō?
Pitri-dhoné bināshoti
rati-mati sob hāriyé āchhō . . .

"Oh wise one, let me hear from you what makes
you qualify as a man? Having squandered all your
inheritance, you are now completely lost . . ."
    As Nabani Bāul's eyes fell on me controlling
the knobs of my tape recorder placed at one side of

the platform, he signalled me to be near him so
that he could find out what I was up to. Nabani
had never seen a tape recorder before. While I
explained, his listeners sat on their benches waiting
patiently for the song to resume:

> . . . Tōmār mondirété nāi-hé Mādhob,
> shāñk phuñké kébol gōl kōrichhō . . .

". . . God is deserting your temple, while you make
noise by blowing conch-shells . . ."

Therefore, when he invited me to visit him in
his village at Siuri, in the district of Birbhum, West
Bengal, I lost no time getting there with my friend
Richard Lannoy one February morning in 1954. I
had my tape recorder and Richard his camera. The
village was green with crystal clear fish ponds, and
the air crisp under the sparkling winter light.

While Nabanidās's songs blended with the
musical landscape of the district of Birbhum, he
himself, with his foot-long plucking drum *Ānan-dalahari* slung on his left shoulder, merged
naturally with the scenery around Siuri as he
walked along his village roads. They were fairly
narrow dirt roads of reddish earth, bordered on
each side by fences made of evergreen shrubs. On
the other side of each fence rested lines of clay
houses with thatched roofs, gently curving down

Nabanidās Bāul (with aektārā) *in Siuri.*

toward the earth. The thatching of the roof was interlaced so tightly with straw and bamboo that, during the monsoon rains, sheets of water rolled down following the curve of the roof, while it provided cool shelter under the harsh sun in summer months.

Some of the houses had their own fish ponds encircled by clusters of banana trees, and patches of flowers and vegetables. And, at not too far a distance surrounding the village, acres of rice fields lay, bordered by coconut and palm trees. As far as the eye could see, the red earth of Birbhum glistened under the winter sun.

Outside Siuri, at one end of the village, Nabani Bāul lived in a couple of huts with his wife and three children—two boys and a girl. Every morning he went out to sing his songs in the village, but only to the houses of his favorite families, and he returned home with uncooked rice and fresh vegetables that were given to him as gifts in exchange for his songs. He alternated his visits to various families so that no household would feel any strain in offering him however modest a gift. What Nabani brought back home at the end of his morning rounds was enough for the family's daily needs, including those of the guests—Richard's and mine.

Purnadās Bāul (with the frame-drum khañjari *and kettle-drum* duggi) *during his tour of France.*

Richard and I were aware of Nabani's situation, although he never said a word about it. Therefore, after about two weeks of staying with his family, when we finally decided to leave for Varanasi, we managed to scrape together a gift of twenty rupees and timidly brought it to him. He looked at Richard, he looked at the money, and then he turned toward me, speaking in a mocking voice: "Well, well, well. How long have you been to London? Have you already forgotten our custom? Tell your friend that I may be a beggar but I don't run a hotel." That was it. Our intention of helping him out a bit in return for his hospitality was nipped in the bud.

Then came the moment of our departure. When Nabanidās saw me struggling under the weight of my tape recorder and the converter for transforming the power from a car battery into 220 A.C., I noticed a twinkle in his laughing eyes. Finally, one day, flaunting his *Ānandalahari* in my face, Nabanidās said, "Well, you too are a wandering Bāul, but unfortunately your instrument is a dead weight." I had, of course, no option but to agree with him that day.

I can't, however, help wondering whether this book would have meant anything to Nabanidās. Possibly not. He could not have read it anyway, since it is written in English. Moreover, he never saw my first book on Bāul songs, also entitled *The Mirror of the Sky,* that was published in 1969 under UNESCO sponsorship. Nabanidās died in 1964, even before his son Purna had become world famous singing Bāul songs that he and his ancestors have been singing for generations in the villages of West Bengal.

Modern literary interest in the works of the Bāuls was aroused by Rabindranath Tagore in 1925, through a lecture at Calcutta University, which was later repeated at Oxford. The poet Tagore is considered one of the pioneers among collectors of Bāul songs. Shri Kshitimohan Sen Shastri, who was a teacher in the poet's Visva Bharati University, is another. Among the later collectors, Professor Upendranath Bhattacharya has fulfilled a remarkable task by publishing a selection of over five hundred songs from his vast collection, together with notes, commentaries, and background history.

Songs of the Bāuls were not conceived for the reading public, nor for literary or artistic reasons. As a matter of fact, most of the Bāuls were unable to read or write, and many of them still are. The texts were created for oral transmission with the aid of music, for religious reasons. The purpose of the songs was sometimes to impart teaching from master to disciple.

The poetic merit of the text is purely incidental, produced by the depth of the Bāul's feelings and his ability to give voice to his intuitions in a simple village language. There is no trace of rationalized "poetic" calculation in the songs of the Bāuls.

The texts which are available today are based on the collection of an individual or of a group of Bāuls, but often incorrectly transcribed by semi-literate hands. The other important source is the living Bāul, but he too has the habit of leaving his own mark on the songs, either deliberately or because of failing memory. The basis of a firm but accurate printed text might be no more than a collector's controversial conjecture.

The translator's task, in this particular case, is made doubly difficult by the added responsibility of having to transpose words of orally transmitted songs into an alien language. A number of the songs, in their original versions, are often concerned with the technical aspect of the Bāul's religious tradition. None of these can be reproduced in word-for-word translation without elaborate explanatory notes. I have included only a few examples of these, mainly concentrating on those that deal with the philosophy of the Bāuls and that can bear the strain of translation. Printed poetry, either original or in translation, ought to be

Nabanidās Bāul, in meditation.

readable without being encumbered by pedantic explanations. In the interest of meaning, I have sometimes had to content myself with fragments or with the addition of a brief commentary on what might otherwise seem obscure.

Starting in 1954, my own tape recordings of the Bāul songs, collected during several years of field work in India, have provided a good deal of material for this as well as my earlier book. The few examples of songs of the Bāuls from Bangladesh that I have included in this volume were recorded in 1971 and the years that followed. During that tragic period, a number of Bāuls, belonging to both the Hindu and the Muslim communities, fled their country, which was then called East Pakistan. They followed the refugees who in the millions escaped to India seeking protection from Pakistan's indiscriminate killing of unarmed Bengali-speaking civilians. This, as we know, resulted in the creation of today's Bangladesh. In 1973, while making a documentary film on the *Bāul Mela*, or annual Bāul fair at Kenduli (Birbhum), I recorded a couple of fascinating Bāul songs that reflected the village life of Bangladesh. These too are included in this volume.

Besides my recorded collection of the Bāul songs, in my selection for rendering into English I have consulted *Bānglār Bāul* by Kshitimohan Sen

Preface

Shastri, Calcutta, 1954; *Lālan Gitikā*, edited by Dr.
Matilal Das and Shri Piyushkanti Mahapatra,
Calcutta, 1958; *Bānglār Palligiti* by Chittaranjan
Dev, Calcutta, 1966; *Bānglār Bāul—Kāvya O
Darshan* by Shri Somendranath Bandopadhyay,
Calcutta, 1964; *Bānglār Sādhak Bāul* by Shrimati
Indira Devi, Calcutta, 1962; and *Bānglār Bāul O
Bāul Gān* by Professor Upendranath Bhattacharya,
Calcutta, 1957.[2]

According to the poetic tradition of Bengal, in
particular that of the Vaishnava poetry, a number of
well-known Bāuls have inserted their names in the
last verse of their songs, making identification
possible. On the other hand, a large number of
songs that are still sung, or those that have been
collected from copyists' notebooks, bear no such
signature lines. These songs are grouped in the first
section and credited as "anonymous" (Anon).

The biographical history of the individual
Bāul, too, is often based on word-of-mouth, and
that also is not always available. Factual infor-
mation such as dates of birth and death, the name
of the village where the Bāul was born, and where
he lived, cannot be traced in a number of cases.
The biographical notes at the end of the book,

[2]For this and much other material concerning the Bāul, I am
deeply indebted to Professor Upendranath Bhattacharya.

therefore, refer only to those about whom the information we have is accepted by specialists.

The songs of the Bāuls explore the worlds of the invisible and the unattainable; they are not merely conventionally organized expressions of feelings illustrated by poetic images. Although some of the songs are a little too long-winded for the purpose of translation, a large selection of these songs are as precise as any expression of poetry and reveal the true creative intuition of the Bāul.

In addition to the voice of the Bāul himself, the songs of the Bāuls have found their way to the lips of the village beggars in Bengal, as also onto city stages through professional singers of traditional songs. In both these cases, music is the main consideration, without having it colored by religious or philosophical pretensions. However, in recent years, since Western intellectuals began to take an interest in the songs of the Bāuls, a new phenomenon in presenting these songs appears to be on the rise. Groups of amateur musicians, donning some sort of fancy robes, purportedly of holy color, can be seen at times on the stages of Paris or London, New York or Los Angeles, presenting themselves as the Bāuls of Bengal. The fact that they have to dress up for the stage to impress their trusting audience cancels their claim to being Bāul. A Bāul is a free spirit. He would not wish to be trapped in a uniform strutting around on a stage. But anyone is free to sing his moving songs to seek the man within.

∽ *Deben Bhattacharya*

TRANSLATOR'S NOTE

In the Introduction that follows, in the section titled *Songs of the Bāuls*, I have discussed the problems I had to face in translating the lyrics. This present note, therefore, is intended to clarify references to God as defined by the Bāul, according to my understanding.

In my translation, God with an upper case "G" represents the Absolute, whereas "the god" (using a lower case "g") stands for the Bāul's personalized vision of the Absolute, although both are one and inseparable to him. Similarly, "Adhar-Mānush," the Unattainable Man, meaning the Absolute, for the Bāul at a sensitive moment of understanding can turn into his personalized vision of the Absolute. I have expressed this through the use of lower case, as in "adhar-mānush," the unattainable man, or "moner-mānush," the man of the heart or the man within.

According to the philosophy of Shri Chaitanya, the Bengali Vaishnava (devotee of Vishnu), a sage and a singer who lived from 1486-1533 C.E., ". . . the god is indivisible. There could be no division between the creator and the created. He is beyond the limits of human thought; that is why this ephemeral world appears neither divided nor undivided from Him."[1] Therefore, according to the Bāul, when God is represented by a name, such as Vishnu, Jesus, or Allah, as also when ascribed a sex, male or female, a worldly attribute, He is neither an image nor a reincarnation. He is God. In the Vedantic literature, however, the Absolute is referred to as "Tat," meaning That, which requires neither a name nor a sex.

[1]Deben Bhattacharya, *Love Songs of Chandidas,* New York: Grove Press, 1970, p. 39.

INTRODUCTION

ॐ

The word Bāul is applied to a small collection of
individuals with a distinctive religious belief,
springing from the village laboring classes—the
intellectually unsophisticated population of Bengal.
To the average Bengali, the Bāul is unconventional
to the degree of being bizarre, yet he demands love
and respect for his songs.

According to his own description of himself,
the Bāul is ". . . wholly dedicated to his own
nature. He laughs or cries, dances or begs as he
wishes . . . He lives a strange life, almost insane,
with values of his own but contrary to others." His
home being under a tree, he moves from district to
district, all the year round, as a dancing beggar
who owns nothing in the world except "a ragged
patch-work quilt."[1]

Even today, in spite of the problems of
partition and poverty, together with rising
industrialization, the Bengalis are avidly interested
in their folk songs and dances, and the village
poetry of socio-religious origin. There are many

[1]Anonymous.

1

varieties of such religious folk expressions, for example, *gambhirā* and *gājan* dances, *jhāpān* and *karam* songs, *pāñchāli* and *bratakathā* poems, etc. These are recited by men and women, in cities as well as in villages, once or more every full moon, depending on the occasion.

An expectant mother will visit the village banyan tree sheltering a clay figure of the goddess *Shashthi* to recite her verses of praise to the goddess in shy whispers, praying for the well-being and health of her forthcoming child. Men, on Saturday evenings, either singly or in a group, will intone the rhymed lines of a long ballad-like text that describes the exploits of Saturn, the astral god who rules the days of the week.

The Bāul can be described as a cultural and religious nomad among the peasant bourgeoisie of Bengal. He uses the peasant language, similes and metaphors:

Cut the rice stalks,
O, rice-growing brother.
Cut them in a bunch
before they begin to smell
rotten like your body
without a living heart.

Introduction .

Sell your goods, my store-keeper brother
while the market is brisk,
when the sun fades
and your customers depart,
your store is a lonely place.

Catch your fish, my fishing-brother,
straining the water off the net.
Once your body begins to rot,
there is neither fish
nor a green leaf,
only an eternally whispering bog.[2]

❧ Anon

The Bāul lives with the peasants, and yet he is
not a peasant. He is not attached to the land. His
songs speak against attachment, to people who
adore their "golden *Bānglā*" lying between the great
Kānchan-janghā peaks in the north and the Bay of
Bengal in the south. Immense rivers, descending
from the Himalayas, weave a network of arteries
across the country until they merge with the ocean.

The climate, tamed and temperate all year
round, bursts into sudden explosions of lightning
and thunder, storms and rains during the summer

---

[2]Tape-recorded at the *Bāul Mela*, Kenduli, Birbhum, 1973. Singer:
Hemanta Bāul from Bangladesh.

monsoon when the warm humid air from the ocean hits the mountain ramparts. The rivers rise up both to destroy and to bring a renewed life to the land. While villages and habitations are wiped out by inundation, forests grow thicker. Stems of jute shoot up, resisting the decaying power of the water, and the rice fields turn golden with the ripening of the paddy corns toward the end of the monsoon.

Fishermen, who have been risking their lives, again set sail on the calm rivers as lines of coconut palms and plantain foliage screen the village. Lotuses flourish on the village pond and the fragrance of the *champak* flower fills the land.

Folk festivities continue throughout the year, at every season, even during the height of the monsoon. The Bengalis have been forced to learn to live with this dual role of the river, destruction with fertility, death with life. These images frequently recur in the Bāul songs:

Never plunge
into the river of lust,
you will not reach the shores.
It is a river of no coasts
where typhoons rage . . .

Dwija Kailāshchandra

Or, while portraying the positive aspect of the
river, the Bāul would sing:

> That enchanting river
> reflects the very form
> of the formless one.
> Sense the essence of the matter . . .
>
> ~ *Gopal*

These themes can be the same from song to
song, or at any rate complementary. The river to
the Bāul is a symbol of life, its two banks
representing birth and death. It can be crossed with
joy only with the help of the man within:

> With no resources of my own
> or any strength of faith,
> my total need requires you ferry me
> over the river of life.
>
> The boat casts off while I stand
> crying on the bank.
> If you smile, my beneficent God,
> your feet will carry me across.

THE MIRROR OF THE SKY

A divided heart is indecisive,
you—my own—may never cross.
Though single-minded, you could walk
to the forecourts of the moon.[3]

◄ *Anon*

The term Bāul connotes a certain madness,
ecstasy, a state of feeling one with the Absolute to
which the Bāul aims. Coming from the rural working
class, drifting from place to place with neither fixed
residence nor personal possessions, he is a
mendicant—but charity towards him is regarded both
by donor and recipient as a reward for artistry. The
songs he sings, the lyrics he composes, which bring
together God with love, life and death, in a simple
unaffected language, attract an attentive audience of
a widely varied background:

Your heart in two measures
will drive you to a dilemma,
Oh, my crazy little heart,
you will never reach the other shore.

[3]Tape-recorded at the *Bāul Melā*, Kenduli, Birbhum, 1973. Singer:
Dilip Bāul.

Single-minded, you will walk
to the court of the Eternal Moon.
but the rich might refuse you entrance
if you were weighed down
by a measuring heart.

The queen of love, Rādhā,
will judge you
before ferrying you across.
Your heart in two measures
will drive you to a dilemma.
Oh, my crazy little heart,
you will never reach the other shore.

A wood-cutter knows no jewel.
None but a jeweller
knows a precious stone.
The goldsmith knows gold
and also the art of polishing it.[4]

≈ *Anon*

The Bāul is undeniably a product of the
Bengali village. His basic personality is deeply
rooted in the land from which he seeks freedom. It
is a conscious enquiry on the part of a simple

[4]Tape-recorded at the *Bāul Melā*, Kenduli, Birbhum, 1973. Singer:
Hemanta Bāul from Bangladesh.

7

peasant mind, and the Bāul brings the physical
world to his aid in his search for the Absolute:

The body of man
is a land for wish-fulfilling—
care will produce
a harvest of jewels.
Plough it in a propitious time.
Hopes that ushered you
to this material world
will bear fruit . . .

ಞ *Kālāchānd*

OUTLINES OF THE HISTORICAL BACKGROUND

The history of Bengal is inextricably entwined with
its ancient folklore since the country never wholly
identified itself with the history of the Aryans, like
the rest of north India. The history of the Bāul is
no exception to this rule. The Sanskrit-speaking
invaders from the north had abruptly stopped at the
border of Bengal for several centuries, viewing the
country with suspicion from neighboring outposts.
It was their first encounter with the northern
Tropics, and they announced that the east was
occupied by huntsmen with strange habits. It was
advisable to call a halt to further advance eastward.

We have no definite information as to the nature of the early Jain and Buddhist contacts with Bengal. If there had been any, the distinguishing marks had already become so faint as to have little bearing on later history.

Therefore, not until the fourth century C.E. did Bengal come under the direct intellectual influence of the Sanskrit mind, while at the same time being politically dominated by the Gupta Empire. The Aryanized history of Bengal begins only from this period. Either as an independent power, or politically controlled, Bengal becomes closely connected with the rest of Sanskrit-speaking India.

The Gupta rule lasted for over two centuries in Bengal. While the ruling classes and the intellectuals became thoroughly involved with the Vedic Hindu culture, which was rapidly absorbing many non-Aryan elements of the region's heritage, the folk religions were given a cloak of Sanskrit respectability. The sturdy fertility goddess of the countryside—or the notoriously self-important Saturn—and many other village gods and goddesses were now endowed with a few verses of praise in Sanskrit in addition to the existing peasant ballads.

Following the end of Gupta rule, Bengal, in the main, continued to be ruled by Hindu kings until the middle of the eighth century, when the country came under the powerful Pāla kings, who were Buddhists. The majority of the population, particularly those of humble origin, adopted the rulers' religion, and Bengal became one of the most important regions for the dissemination of Buddhist idcals. The Pālas ruled till the middle of the twelfth century, when they were replaced by the Senas, the Vaishnava Hindus from the south. The Sena reign lasted for a little over one hundred years.

By the close of the thirteenth century, the whole of Bengal was in Muslim hands; fanatical efforts at proselytizing the Hindus and Buddhists to Islam followed. This had an important bearing on the development of the Bāul tradition as we know it today. In addition to the village laboring classes among the Hindus and the Buddhists, a large number of Muslims, presumably some of those converted during the Islamic expansion in Bengal and a certain section of the Sufis, the mystics of Islam, took to the Bāul faith.

The Muslim domination of Bengal ended with British rule, and the history of British India has no direct relationship to the history of the Bāuls.

Introduction

THE BĀUL FAITH

The distinctive quality of the Bāul religious thought lies in its robust simplicity and in its directness of expression:

> When the life,
> the mind
> and the eyes
> are in agreement,
> the target is
> within your reach:
> you can see
> the formless *Brahma*
> with bare eyes . . .
>
>   *Hāude Gosāiñ*

The Bāul accepts that God is formless, but to him the form and the formless are one and inseparable; therefore, what matters most to the Bāul is the interrelationship between God and existence, the universe:

> . . . Forget not
> that your body contains
> the whole of existence.
>
>   *Gosāiñ Gopāl*

11

In his attitude to God and the universe, the Bāul is closer to the *Tantras*, the system parallel to the *Vedas* of Hindu religious thought. The *Vedas* were brought by the Aryans, and in general deal with the gods related to nature, such as the sun, the rains and so on, and mainly portray the masculine world of tough herdsmen. The *Tantras*, on the other hand, reflect the ancient folklore of the land which is part of pre-Aryan belief, though discreetly Aryanized. It deals with the domain of the mind, the known and the unknown spheres of human psychology, and masculine power and female energy both in sex and the search for God. In the *Tantras*, the worlds of god, demon and man, the abstract and the tangible, are all but reflections of the same vital force:

> All physical and mental forms, everything in the universe, is that one, appearing in various ways. Life is one, all its forms are interrelated in a vastly complicated but inseparable whole. Every act by any form of life, from the highest to the lowest, must react on every other form. We are but links in a long series. We are made of the same substance as the stars, the same substance as the gods.[5]

[5] Ajit Mukerjee, *Tantra Art*, Kumar Gallery, Paris-New York-New Delhi, 1966.

12

Introduction

The *Tantras* are rather harsh, like surgical knives. They take the impulses into account only in order to be free from the pressure of passions. They have little patience for the emotional sublimation of the impulses, such as love, which does not strike the *Tantra* mind as reliable. Whereas to the Bāul, love is nearly a synonym for God:

Lust and love
and the erotic acts
are housed in one single place . . .

                Hāude Gosāiñ

Owing to his lack of conventionality, the Bāul is able to surpass even himself in his directness of expression:

The essence of love
lies in carnal lust
bearing a deep secret.
Only lovers
can unravel it . . .

                Chandidās Gosāiñ

This emphasis on love in the Bāul literature suggests the influence of the Vaishnava religious tradition, which overtook Bengal during the leadership of Shri Chaitanya Deva (1486-1533 C.E.). According to Shri Chaitanya, God is indivisible. There is no separation between the creator and the created. A devotee must utilize the compulsive power of his own emotion in trying to find union with God. And in loving God, he must be free from any motive other than the act of loving. But Shri Chaitanya did not take the physical impulses of love into account, whereas the *Tantra* did. And so did the Bāul.

The Bāul combined Shri Chaitanya's path of devotion with the *Tāntrik* realism. Therefore, he could say with conviction:

Release the sensation
of taste
on your tongue.
Open the doors of feelings . . .
Lust and love
and the erotic acts
are housed in one single place
where sorrows and joys
do not exist . . .

       Hāude Gosāiñ

At the same time, the Bāul could find himself
sharing Shri Chaitanya's devotion and express
himself with the lyricism of the Vaishnava poetry:[6]

I am fulfilled
being the breath you blow
on your flute . . .
What more could I wish
than to dissolve
in the breath of your melody?

∽ Ishān Jugi

It should be possible to draw comparisons
between the Bāul ideas and a number of existing
philosophies in India as well as with Sufi mysti-
cism. Indeed, the quotation below of a poem by the
Persian Sufi poet Jalalu'l-din Rumi has a striking
resemblance, both in the poetic context as well as
in devotional feeling, with the above-quoted Bāul
song.

We have already seen that the Bāuls come
from both the Hindu and the Muslim communities

---

[6]Deben Bhattacharya, *Love Songs of Chandidās*, London, 1967.
Chandidās is considered the father of the Bengali Vashnava
poetry on the theme of Rādhā and Krishna's romance. This
theme, as a subject for poetry, became extremely popular in
Bengal following the Vaishnava religious movement, which was
sparked off by Shri Chaitanya Deva during the sixteenth century.

in Bengal. It is quite usual for a Muslim Bāul to have a Hindu teacher or vice versa, and for a Hindu Bāul to sing on Islamic themes, or the other way round. To the Bāul, the conventions of Islam and Hinduism are equally neutral. But it would run contrary to principle if they were to break away from the established institutions only to set up a new one for Bāuls alone. Therefore, they chose to remain inhabitants of the no-man's land between these two religious communities.

Poetic mysticism is universal, but is particularly refined in a number of religions, both in the East and the West. Among them the Mevlevi Dervish movement, which sprang from Sufism and developed in Turkey under the Persian Sufi poet Jalalu'l-din Rumi toward the second half of the thirteenth century, was possibly the closest to the ways of the Bāul in employing poetry, music, and dance as mediums for prayer. This was indeed an act of rebellion against the orthodox interpretation of the Koranic laws, which forbids music and dance in places of worship. Jalalu'l-din Rumi (1207-1273 C.E.), in his famous *Mathnawi*, describes the soul's liberation from self while it is filled with the love of God:

Listen to the reed breathing
Fervent love and intense pain
Since it was wrenched
From its marshy bed . . .

Kindled by the spark of love,
I am drunk with love's own wine.
If you wish to know what lovers suffer
Listen to the reed.[7]

∾ Rumi

It is tempting to compare Rumi's statement, "Feel that you yourself [are] God . . .,"[8] with the Hindu belief in the Vedantic expression *soham*, meaning "I am That," the Absolute being referred to as "That" instead of being qualified by a name. The Bāul calls it the *Moner-Mānush*, "the Man within," or the *Adhar-Mānush*, the "Unattainable Man," a symbol for the Absolute that is free from attributes or the limitations of the sexes. The Absolute is neither male nor female, but both:

[7]I. Mathnawi, adapted from the poem "The Song of the Reed," Reynold A. Nicholson, *RUMI—Poet and Mystic, 1207-1273*, London, 1956, p. 31.
[8]Quoted in *MEVLÂNA*, Mevlāna Tertip Heyeti Reisi, Konya, 1959, p. 31.

17

... The man or the woman
is still alone,
but a lover is formed
when the souls conjoin ...

         ∾ *Manohar*

Dervish songs have been written by a number
of mystical poets, such as Yunus Emre, who also
lived in Turkey during the thirteenth century:

Together with the mountains and stones,
I call you, my Lord,
And with the birds at dawn,
I call you, my Lord.

In the sky with Jesus Christ,
And on Mount Sinai with Moses
Holding his staff in his hand,
I call you, my Lord . . .[9]

         ∾ *Yunus Emre*

Similarly, St. John of the Cross in his "Songs
of the Soul in Rapture" treats God with the
devotion of a lover:

[9]Tape-recorded in Ankara in 1972. Singer: Ahmet Hatipoglu.

18

... Within my flowering breast
which only for himself entire I save
He sank into his rest
And all my gifts I gave
Lulled by the airs with which the cedars
wave.[10]

The *Rig Veda*, the earliest sacred text of India,
compiled approximately 1500 B.C.E. or earlier, also
occasionally refers to the god with friendly
intimacy:

In your boat, my lord,
you and I, the two close friends,
were afloat on the sea.
Why do you wish to destroy me now?
Where has our friendship gone?[11]

But the Bāul has a sturdier approach to the
Almighty. With his firm belief that a god is housed
within himself, he finds that there is little use in
projecting his complaints outward. Instead, he
challenges the god:

---

[10]*St. John of the Cross*, translated by Roy Campbell, London, 1960.
[11]*Rig Veda* 7.88. 3-5.

You may hurt me, my lord,
go, hurt me
as long as I can bear the pain.

≈ *Podu*

Some scholars have attempted to connect the
Bāul belief mainly with Vedic thought,[12] but the
arguments in favor of the suggestion are not
convincing. The *Vedas* were occupied with estab-
lishing the Hindu religious rites and the sanctity of
the Brahmanic hierarchy against which, similar to
the Buddhists, the Bāuls rebelled. Though most
Indian thought could be compared, one way or
another, with the vast Vedic literature that had
accumulated over many centuries, the Vedic poetry
is far too abstract and dry to inspire the rise of the
Bāul tradition, which springs from the heart. For
example, while comparing the relationship between
life and death, the *Rig Veda* says:

Life lives on the dead,
Life and death spring from the same
source.[13]

---

[12]Kshitimohan Sen Shartri, *Bānglar Bāul,* Calcutta, 1954.
[13]*Rig Veda* 1. 164. 30.

The theme of life and death is extremely
urgent with the Bāul too, but his approach to the
problem is completely different from that of the
herdsmen who had to live from their cattle. The
Bāul interpretation of the question is less didactic
and severe. His enquiry, instead of emphasizing the
means for being alive, treats God, the "Man of the
heart," as the focal point:

> . . . the Man you seek
> is earthed
> in the earth,
> deceased while being.
>
> Dying with death,
> you must live to seek . . .
>
> ᴥ *Anon*

The Vedic statement is connected with the
tangible, that which can be rationally explained.
The Bāul's search is for the intangible, which
dwells within a rational state of being. The god is
in everything—therefore, he is in life and in death,
and as the god is within the Bāul's being, the Bāul
cannot separate life from death, nor death from life.
The scholastic explanation of the Bāul's approach
to life's relationship to death is that the soul is

allied to the self. The soul lives, but the ego must
die for the development of the Bāul:

> . . . He who is able
> to be born
> at the door of death,
> is devoted eternally . . .
> Die before dying,
> die living.

≈ Gosāiñ Gopāl

Studying the Bāul songs we find that the main
theme—the interrelationship of forms, physical and
mental—is wholly submerged within the formless,
"the One who moves close to his hands but away
from his reach." Therefore, the Formless is the
form, and the visible form the Formless, beyond
the senses of perception.

Rationalization is an inadequate tool when
dealing with the intangible. It is like a lover trying
to analyze why he has fallen in love—by the time
he has found an explanation, the feeling of love has
been lost. Our life is balanced on this tightrope of
knowing entwined with unknowing, of life with
death, or of being locked within oneself while
being free to accept that "lust and love and the
erotic acts are housed in one place."

In assessing the rise and development of the Bāul philosophy, we find that, true to the Bāul belief, it drew life from anything that was available to it: the ancient pre-Aryan folklore of Bengal; the *Tantras* which can be described as the correlated system of certain pre-Aryan and Aryan beliefs; the *Vedas*; the Buddhist rebellion against the Brahmanic intellectual authority; the Vaishnava movement of Shri Chaitanya; and the introduction of Sufi mysticism following Islamic rule. The Bāul is not an intellectual, but he has a natural wisdom and a feeling for the simple and the direct. Though he could not read the doctrines, he was able to select their essentials. The process of assimilation started with the principle of discarding the organized system while accepting the faith.

To the Bāul, who is an individualist by nature, faith is spontaneous because it springs from trust. It is related to the *Adhar-Mānush*, the "Unattainable Man" who dwells in the human form. The "system," on the other hand, controls the spirit of man in order to possess a large number of individuals within its orbit. To the Bāul, an individual's feelings for the *Adhar-Mānush* spring directly from faith. An organized system produces habits and customs that are not congenial to the Bāul priority of alertness to the "Man of the heart." Formalities become more important than the god:

The god is deserting your temple
as you amuse yourself
by blowing conch-shells
and ringing bells . . .

       ~ Padmalochan

Thus, in his search for God, the Bāul is a determined individualist who passionately rejects any organized system. The system stands in his way as threateningly as a roadblock:

The road to you is blocked
by temples and mosques.
I hear your call, my lord,
but I cannot advance—
prophets and teachers
bar my way . . .

       ~ Madan

God, to the Bāul, is everywhere, therefore nowhere outside himself. The Bāul is always struggling to overcome his ego which separates him from the "Man of the heart":

A man unknown to me
and I,
we live together
but in a void,
a million miles
between us . . .

         ❧ *Lālan*

And yet, like a difficult lover, God is present at home and away, near and far, in scepticism and trust, in desire and in feeling, in life and in death, all at once. The Bāul songs reflect the Bāul's efforts in adjusting himself to the concept of freedom while accepting the bondage of the skin and bones.

SONGS OF THE BĀULS

Even if you forbid,
dear friend,
I am helpless;
my songs contain
my prayers.

Some flowers pray
through the radiance
of their colors
and others, being dark,
with fragrance.
As the *vinā* prays
with its vibrating strings,
do I with my songs.

~ Madan

The oldest of the Bāul songs that are available
today were created during the eighteenth century.
The Bāul did not write down his songs, either
because he was incapable of doing so or because
he did not feel any urge to make his creation perm-
anent. Since he did not believe in propaganda or
conversion, he made his songs for himself, and at
times as teachings to his disciples—his own way of
coming to terms with himself with regard to the
god and love, life and death, society and the
individual.

The songs do not show any trace of collective
thinking on the part of the Bāul, nor is there any
suggestion of preaching. These are composed by
individuals, in simple village language, using
regional vocabulary and intonations from different
parts of Bengal. The images portrayed in the songs

Bāul instruments.

refer to village scenes, professions of the inhab-
itants, and objects used in everyday life. The songs
could be grouped to represent the following
subjects:

- Appeals to the teacher and the enquiry
  into God.
- Inner union with God—"the Man of
  the heart," "the Unattainable Man."
- Metaphysical analysis of the human
  body and the material world.
- Physical and mental disciplines for
  spiritual development.
- Questions regarding life and death and
  the understanding of death while being
  fully alive.
- Futility of doctrinaire social and
  religious systems and the traditions of
  caste, class, and race.

From the point of view of written poetry and
its technique, the Bāuls have little to offer. The
vocabulary is colloquial and limited. Often, the
rhythmic structures of the verses are slack, mono-
tonous and impetuous. Obviously, the words of the
songs have been put together not for the rhythm of
the poetry, but with the melody of the song in
mind. As a result, an extra syllable or two, here

Ānandalahari.

and there, have been prolonged or shortened according to the need of the melody. Following the tradition of Bengali poetry of the period, the verses are usually rhymed. The meters employed by the Bāul spring mainly from village poetry and Vaishnava poems,[14] but as can be seen from the following example, the Bāul leaves his own mark on the meter. This particular meter, entitled *dhāmāli*, is fairly popular with the Vaishnava poets. It is even in its metric structure, and the time-division of each line consists of 4+4+4+2. The following quotation from a song by the Bāul, Bishā Bhuñimāli, shows how flexible is the Bāul's use of an accepted metrical form. While he maintains the set time-division in the first half of the stanza, in the second half he takes advantage of the Bāul's usual privilege—the freedom of action:

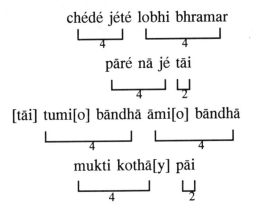

---

[14]*cf.* Note 6, page 15 re. *Love Songs of Chandidās.*

Aektārā with a pair of āndalaharis. Bāul fair at Kenduli.

The extra syllables used by the Bāul Bishā
Bhuñimāli are placed in brackets. The words of the
quotation mean:

> The bee is avid
> and unable to leave.
> So, you are bound
> and I am bound—
> where is freedom then?

Generally speaking, the songs are sung with
the accompaniment of instrumental music. The
instruments of the Bāul are:

(1) The *gopijantra* or the *aektārā*. A one-
stringed drone instrument. The string is plucked by
a wire plectrum fitted to the index finger. The belly
of the instrument is made of an open-headed cala-
bash, and the neck is a meter-long bamboo that is
split down the middle. Each half of the split
bamboo neck is then fixed symmetrically to the
open end of the gourd.

(2) The next in importance is the *ānandalahari*,
or onomatopoeically speaking, the *gubgubi*. It is a
plucking drum with a pair of gut-strings attached to
the inside of the skin of a foot-long, single- headed
drum. The other ends of the strings are fixed to a
small drum, not bigger than a coffee cup. This
small drum, held in the left hand of the drummer,

Nabanidās Baul, singing in Siuri.

keeps the gut-strings taut while the big drum, hanging from his left shoulder, is kept tightly pressed under his arm. By contracting and relaxing the strings, the Bāul controls the variation of the pitch while striking them with a plectrum. Dexterous use of the plectrum introduces a variety of timbres and rhythms.

(3) *Dotārā*. A four-stringed long-necked lute. The belly of the instrument is covered with goat skin. The lute is played with a plectrum. This instrument is extremely popular in different types of folk music all over Bengal.

(4) *Duggi*. A kettle-drum. It is tied to the Bāul's waist as he plays it with one hand and accompanies himself on the drone instrument, *gopijantra*, with the other, while dancing.

(5) *Juri* is a pair of small bell-metal cymbals.

Poetry, music, song, and dance are the tools that the Bāul uses for his vocation. But all these forms of expression are devoted to enquiries into man's relationship with God, the purpose of existence as man being:

O my senseless heart,
you have failed to cultivate
the human-land . . .
Cultivated,
it would have yielded a harvest of gold . . .

❧ Anon

Most of the Bāul songs are based on the
enquiry into oneself and one's relationship with the
god. As we have discussed the subject earlier in
detail, we shall concentrate here on the technical as
well as the social aspects of the Bāul songs.

The Bāul earns his living mostly from his
songs, singing from door to door. Donations are
considered a form of charity in Bengal, but with
dignity on the part of the collector. When singing
alone in front of a village audience, the Bāul sings,
dances, and plays the string drone, *gopijantra*, and
the kettle-drum, *duggi*. The clusters of small bells
tied round his ankles give the rhythm of his dance.
The melodies of the Bāul's songs are often a
blending of two or more tunes, and are rooted in
the regional folk music of Bengal, with a distinc-
tive form and a style of his own. This style is so
individualistic that it has come to be known as the
Bāul sur, the melody of the Bāul. When singing in
a group, the Bāul uses other instruments as well.

His voice is not always melodious or pleasant
to listen to. During my recording of Nabanidās
Bāul in his village in Birbhum, Nabanidās had lost
his voice owing to an overdose of hemp that he
had been smoking before he started singing.
There was a small crowd in a sweet shop in Siuri,
listening to him. The audience did not care about
the quality of his voice, as he was able to com-
municate to his listeners naturally, effortlessly.
Through his songs, Nabanidās directed his
questions and answers to himself, and yet he was
able to stir every single individual in this village
gathering. The audience sat spellbound, listening,
asking him to sing over and over again. One of his
songs started with this challenging note:

What makes you think
that you are human?
Having squandered
your heritage of heart,
you are not lost in lust . . .

≈ *Padmalochan*

Neither the singer nor the audience could be described as sophisticated, but no one took any notice of the tape recorder. Yet, they were wholly involved in the theme of the song, with every word of it. An Indian audience is usually critical of the timbre or the quality of the voice, but when it comes to songs of introspective nature, they can easily become involved with the spirit of the text. If the singer has a hoarse voice because of a cold or for some other reason, the audience is understanding. But if it is purely art music, the audience can be as unkind as in any city of the world.

The Bāul tradition spread all over Bengal. More than forty famous Bāuls and a large number of anonymous ones have emerged since the beginning of the eighteenth century.

Socially, the Bāul tradition can be interpreted as a collection of isolated individualists in rebellion against caste and class systems. It started as a revolt against the conventions of the established religions, such as Islam and the Hindu faith, while being involved with both. Though infrequently, the Bāul has also taken the prevalence of social inequality to task:

. . . the rites of spring
have burst in the Tāj Mahal.
Little sons of pigs
who were ruled by the powerful king
have gone out of control
taking charge of all.

The rites of spring
have burst in the Tāj Mahal.

Anon

There can be nothing more revolutionary than
the idea of holding a spring festival in the Tāj
Mahal, the very seat of Islamic Imperial Power.
The *dol*, or the color festival of the springtime, is
essentially Hindu and is alien to orthodox Islam.

For a people of restrained rural life and almost
negligible literary training, the Bāul has a unique
sensibility. Since he accepts nothing which is
offered to him ready-made, he discards nothing that
he can translate into the Bāul language. Here is a
Bāul song portraying the modern age with the
images of the mechanized world, but rendered into
the Bāul idiom:

Introduction

If you wish to board an airplane
you must travel light,
to be safe from the danger of a crash.
You must renounce
your errors and inhibitions . . .

‮~‬ *Anon*

THE SONGS

Scanning the cosmos
you waste your hours:
he is present
in this little vessel.

He does not dwell
in the complex of stars
nor in limitless space;
he is not found
in the ethical scriptures
nor in the text of the *Vedas.*[1]
He lives beyond the existence
of all.

He[2] is here
in his form without form
to adorn the hamlet of limbs,
and the sky above
is the globe of his feelings
the platform of spontaneous matter.

      Anon

[1]The *Vedas* constitute the earliest available sacred texts of India.
Four in number, they are *Rigveda, Yajurveda, Sāmaveda* and
Atharvaveda. While the first three are available in their entirety,
Atharvaveda exists only in fragments and quotations. The
assessed dates about the *Vedas* vary widely, from 3000 B.C.E. to
1500 B.C.E.
[2]God, unattainable by the senses, formless.

The mirror of the sky
reflects my soul.
O Bāul of the road,
O Bāul, my heart,
what keeps you tied
to the corner of a room?

As the storm rampages
in your crumbling hut,
the water rises to your bed.
Your tattered quilt
floats on the flood,
your shelter is down.

O Bāul of the road,
O Bāul, my heart,
what keeps you tied
to the corner of a room?

↜ *Anon*[1]

---

[1]Written down from the collection of an itinerant Bāul in
Varanasi.

All of us
in our different ways
think of God.
He is the dispenser of love,
beyond senses and feelings.

And yet,
it is only in the essence of loving
that God is found.

✍ Anon

Attested by your own heart,
O my Master,
lead me the right way
as you play the melody
on the lute.
The lute could never sing
on its own
without you to play it.

✍ Anon

Your form is composed
of the five elements,[1]
do not ignore them.
With your mind
tune the *vina*'s strings
that give a sweet melody.

≈ *Anon*

[1]The five elements: earth, water, fire, air, and ether.

Whom will you regard
as your teacher, O my heart,[1]
and bow in reverence?
A teacher is a guest
in your home
and a traveller on the road.
Countless are the teachers, my heart,
for bowing in reverence.

The teacher is you offering dignity to all
and to the agony of death.
The teacher is the suffering in your heart
that makes you weep.
To whom will you bow in reverence,
my heart?

~ *Anon*

[1]*Mon*, from the Sanskirt *manas*; in colloquial Bengali it implies
both heart and mind; to the Bāul it represents himself,
symbolizing heart and mind, spirit and matter.

The ways of the tortuous river[1]
slip from your grasp.
Brothers, beware,
do not step into the stream.

The water rushes down
wrecking the blackened hills.
Brothers, beware
of the tortuous stream.

The river was dry
when the waters of the flood
surged down the twisting river bed.
How can we cross the river now?

Be on your guard, O boatman,
hold tight to the oars.
And if the boat[2] threatens disaster,
remember the Master.

Anon

[1]River, symbol for life.
[2]Boat, symbol for the human body.

Only an adept
in the flavors of love
can comprehend
the language of a lover's heart,
others have no clue.

The taste of lime
rests in the core of the fruit,
and even experts know
of no easy way
to reach it.

Honey is hidden
within the lotus bloom—
but the bee knows it.
Dung-beetles nestle in dung,
discounting honey.

The forest of Brindā[1]
guards the essence of love—
Rādhā and Krishna,
with cowherds ruling the land.

Submission is the secret of knowledge.

Anon

[1]Brindāban, a town in north India where Krishna spent his days as a youth.

Mad, mad,
we are all mad.
Why is this word
so derogatory then?
Diving deep into the heart's stream
you will find
that no one is better
than the one who is mad.

Some are mad after wealth
and others for glory.
Some go mad
with poverty,
others with aesthetic forms
and the flavors of feelings.
Some are madly in love.
And some of those who go mad
only laugh or cry.
The glamor of madness is great.

Mad, mad!
Madness does not grow
on the tree,
but only when
fake and fact
are meaningless,
and all, being equal,
are bittersweet.

❧ Anon

The rites of spring
have burst in the Tāj Mahal.
The meaning of the words
right and wrong,
life and death,
are cast away into the empty space
of meaninglessness.

The rites of spring
have burst in the Tāj Mahal.
Little sons of pigs
who were ruled by the powerful king
have gone out of control
taking charge of all.

The rites of spring
have burst in the Tāj Mahal.

✎ *Anon*[1]

[1]Tape-recorded in Calcutta, 1954. Singers: Ramakrishna Bāul
Sangha, Howrah.

THE MIRROR OF THE SKY

According to the views of the world,
there is no one so undesirable and unworthy
    as he.
His heart locked with feelings,
he is as gay as a whirligig to the outside
    world.
Cleaving wholly to his own nature,
he laughs or cries, dances or begs.
Regardless of cleanliness or impurity,
good or evil,
his heart is carved in stone,
but his life is a joy.

People grind their teeth at him,
turn him away from their doorsteps
when he goes begging for a handful of
    rice.
He has no right to talk back
as he must discard all for the sake of God,
accepting all as part of divine caprice.

A tramp by nature and a beggar at that,
he lives a strange life, almost insane,
with values of his own which are contrary
to those of others.
His home being under a tree,
he moves from district to district
all the year round,
as a dancing beggar who owns nothing
     in the world
but a ragged patchwork quilt.

✍ Anon

Nothing has happened
and nothing will happen.
what is there,
is there.

I became a king
in my dream
and my subjects
occupied the entire earth.
I sat on the throne
ruling like a lion,
living a happy life.
The world obeyed me.

As I turned in my bed,
all was clear:
I was not a lion
but a lion's uncle,
a jackass,
the village idiot.

 Anon

Commit yourself to the earth
while on earth,
my heart,
if you wish to attain
the unattainable man.[1]
Place at his feet
your flowers of feelings
and the prayers of tears
flooding your eyes.

The man you seek
is on earth,
in the earth,
deceased yet being.

Dying with death,
you must live to seek.

          Anon

---

[1]God, unattainable by the senses, formless.

Come if you wish to meet
the new man.
He has abandoned
his worldly possessions
for the beggar's sack
that hangs from his shoulder.
He speaks of the eternal mother
[Kāli, the goddess of time]
even as he enters the Ganges.

Simple words can overcome
ignorance and disbelief:
Kāli and Krishna are one.
The words may differ—
the meaning is precisely the same.
He who has broken
the barrier of words
has conquered limitations:
Allah or Jesus, Moses or Kāli,
the rich or the poor,
sage or fool,
all are one and the same to him.

Lost in his thoughts,
to others he seems insane.
He opens his arms
to welcome the world,
calling all to the ferry boat
tied to the coast of life.

               ≈ Anon[1]

[1]Tape-recorded in Calcutta, 1954. Singers: Ramakrishna Bāul
Sangha, Howrah.

Raise the torch of love
as high as the lightning
to discern precious gold
from common tin.

Words of wisdom
describing God
can reveal no riches
in a darkened room.
Seeking in darkness
is confusing . . .

Break the barriers,
the nights of darkness,
and look at the sky:
the formless, beautiful,
is held in the arms of the moon.[1]

              ≈ *Anon*

[1]*Chandra, chānd* and *Krishnachandra*—the moon and the black moon—represent Krishna, God.

. . . The potter
cuts the clay
and kneads it
and shapes it
with elegance.

Impure gold
holds no color on its own.
You must burn it in the fire
for purity
and color . . .

                           ❧ *Anon*

O my senseless heart,
you have failed to cultivate
the human-land.
How will you face the tax claims
when the season wanes?
You have no balance
to your credit at all.

As you wonder, sitting alone,
the time approaches for death,
heedless of all.
O my insane heart,
you have travelled
eight million times
the painful ways of life to death,[1]
to find the measured land,
the body of the man.
Why did you let such human-earth
turn to wasteland?
Cultivated,
it could have yielded a harvest of gold.

Take up, my heart,
the spade of devotion—
wrench out the weeds of sin.
The seed of faith will grow.[2]

Passions within you
are feeding on you.
They will never let you act.
Leave them and worship
Shri Gaurānga's[3] feet,
the root of devotion and love.

Anon[4]

[1]These lines relate to the concept of reincarnation: spiritual
development through rebirth.

[2]*Bījamantra*, seed-word or charged word: selected letters from the
Sanskrit alphabet given by the guru to a disciple. By
concentrating on and repeating the *mantra* the disciple is helped
to coordinate his physical, mental, and psychic nature.

[3]Shri Gaurānga refers to Shri Chaitanya Deva, the sixteenth
century Vaishnava teacher from Nabadwip, West Bengal, as a
fair-skinned man.

[4]Tape-recorded in Siuri, Birbhum, in 1954. Singer: Purna
Chandra, son of Nabanidās Bāul.

When a girl leaves
her childhood home
to make her nest
with an unknown man,
she sheds her tears,
she laughs and smiles.
Though great is the union,
love is a tie.

~ Anon

Lust is iron
Love, gold.

~ Anon

You must be single-minded
to visit the court of my Gaurchānd.[1]
If your mind is torn in two
you will swim in a quandary
and never reach the shore.

The court has ordered the queen of love,
Rādhā, to ferry all across,
but after the mind is measured.
The jewellers who weigh are strict
and the scales are accurate.

A woodcutter is no judge
of precious stones;
the ox that carries the sweet-maker's load
knows no taste of sugar.
Gold is known to the goldsmith
as also the art of testing it.

Anon[2]

[1]Gaurchānd, the fair-moon, is an endearing popular name in Bengal for Shri Chaitanya Deva, the sixteenth century Vaishnava teacher from Nabadwip, West Bengal.
[2]Tape-recorded in Siuri, Birbhum, 1954. Singer: Nabanidās Bāul. Recorded again at the annual Bāul Fair in Kenduli, Birbhum, in 1973. Singer: Hemanta Bāul.

Planting the tree of hope,
I sat in its shade
waiting for fruits.
But the branches broke
before the tree could bear:
barren were my hopes.

The rain-bird[1] flies towards the clouds,
but the clouds glide away
to another land.

ᐭ Anon

The *Vedas* bear a wealth of wisdom—
of that I am convinced.
But the author of my book
has abandoned his pen,
lacking that inward flow.

ᐭ Anon

---

[1]In Indian poetry and painting the *chātaka (Hierococcyx varius)* is depicted as the bird that is intensely in love with the clouds, as it is supposed to live on rain water.

What dealings
can you conclude
with someone
who is unaware
of the feelings
in loving?

A blind burglar
trying to steal
bores a hole
through the wrong wall.
He risks his life
laboring in vain—
the fate of the blind
taps no treasures.
The owl
stares at the sky,
sitting blind
to the rays of the sun . . .

Anon

. . . He is watching the path
with a balance in hand.
Be bold, my heart,
and enter the territory
of the great
by daring the unconquerable.
Let desires be at your will,
obeying you.

The path is perilous:
a narrow raft
divides the wild waters of the sea.
And submarine chains
bar the way
to the rowing boats.

You must also cross
the moat of fire,
and walk on the edge of a sword
in steady steps.
Below you lie the death of pain
and a raging furnace . . .

Give up excuses,
seek energy in wisdom:
find strength
in the force of a lotus bloom.

Anon

Dear love,
you who share my pain
can tell me why my heart
is lost to listlessness
and walks by itself
toward its self
without commotion.

There is no patience
in the core of my heart—
shivering with tears
it cries with the eyes,
and in the silence of lovely sound
forever calls:
come, please come.

Anon

What color is your cottage
on the shore of this bogus world?
The frame of your home is made of bones
and the roof is thatched with skin.
But the pair of peacocks
on the landing-pier
hardly know that
they will end one day.

As childhood is passed in play
so passes the game of passion.
Old age, too, is a going-away,
calling, calling
for the master and the lord.
Your teeth are dropping
and your hair grows grey.
The age of manhood
is at a low ebb.
The plaster of your painted home
will be crumbling, now:
softly, softly . . .

Anon[1]

[1]Tape-recorded in Calcutta in 1954. Singer: Abbass-uddin, the late professional singer of folk songs from Bangladesh (East Bengal).

If you wish to board an airplane
you must travel light,
to be safe from the danger of a crash.
You must renounce
your errors and inhibitions
and show your credentials at the airport.
Paying your fare of devotion to God,
you must give up
your worldly wealth
to buy a ticket for a seat.
The feet of your Master,
the airplane,
will take you to Vishnu's sphere[1]
in less than an eyelid's wink . . .

Anon[2]

[1]Vishnu is the preserving power of the Hindu triple forces, the
other two being Brahmā, creation, and Shiva, dissolution.
[2]Tape-recorded in Varanasi in 1954. Singer: Haripada Debnath.

That astounding engine
of the train[1]
makes the wheels move
with organized power
drawn from the beautiful earth—
fire, water and air.

But the day comes when
the passenger leaves,
and the boiler breaks down
and the engine stops
and four shoulders
bear the machinery
to the funeral ground.
And all for the astounding engine
of the train.

             Anon

[1]The body.

A group of young singers of Bāul songs.
Bāul fair at Kenduli.

Who gave shape
to such a splendid room[1]
with astonishing workmanship?
The master-builder
merits my gratitude,
but where does he himself live?

The room erected
on three columns[2]
is a network
of rope, cord and string.[3]
It has nine standard doors[4]
but the windows[5]
are countless.
The span of the room,
fourteen quarter-measures,[6]
can contain
full fourteen worlds.[7]

Amazing workmanship
of the master-mechanic!
The room revolves
and halts on its own—
mobility alternates
with motionlessness.

Talking earth
walling my room
holds fire and water
in a united stream,
flushing the floor.
In my room
live in total unity
the sage and the thief,
the demon and the man,—
poison and nectar.

∼ *Ananta*

[1] The body.
[2] The two legs and the spinal column of the physical body, and the *idā, pingalā,* and *sushumnā,* vessels of the spiritual body.
[3] Blood vessels, arteries, veins.
[4] The nine forces of perception and action: ears, skin, eyes, nose, anus, genital organ, hands, feet, and the tongue representing the double function of tasting and speaking.
[5] The pores of the skin.
[6] *Choudda poyā* (fourteen quarters): popular expression for three and a half times the length of a person's forearm, which is considered to be the approximate height of a man or a woman.
[7] The seven nether worlds represented by the lower half of the human body, and the six heavenly spheres and the earth represented by the upper half.

O, my heart,
let us go then,
let us walk
to the grove
of Krishna's love.
The breeze
of joy
will calm
your life.

In that woodland
eternally bloom
five scented flowers.[1]
Their fragrance
will enchant
your life and soul,
giving them
sovereign dignity.

Ananta

[1]The five elements: earth, water, fire, air, and ether.

The heart, a lotus,
continues flowering
age after age.
You are bound to it
and so am I
with no escape.

The lotus blossoms,
blossoms, blossoms—
there is no end to it—
but all have one type of honey
with one particular taste.

The bee is avid
and unable to leave.
Thus, you are bound
and I am bound.
Where is freedom then?

      Bishā Bhuñimāli

The essence of love
lies in carnal lust
bearing a deep secret.
Only lovers
can unravel it.

      Chandidās Gosāiñ

Each fruit is open to
two frontiers
and borne on
a pair of trees.[1]
Deep meditation
reveals the knowledge
beyond any doubt.

The two
who are wholly present
can bring forth a fruit
to offer the Master.
They are conscious
and fruitful.

Darkness and copper:[2]
the well never sinks
into the water.

            Chandidās Gosāiñ

[1]The male and the female elements.
[2]Offering of copper to the darkness implies that the darkness is a
blessing for the well.

Let ripeness appear
in its own time
for the full flavor
of the fruit.
A green jackfruit
can be softened by blows
but not made sweet.

             Chandidās Gosāiñ

The milk of the lioness
is seen at its best
when stored in a golden cup.
Worshipping prospers
in a proper container.

The lover
who wholly loves
can reach reality,
comprehending the unattainable man.[1]
The secrets of death
are revealed to him
while he is fully alive.
What does he care
for the other shores of life?

             Chandidās Gosāiñ

[1]God, unattainable by the senses, formless.

Human limbs
are held together
by a pair of lotus blooms[1]
growing in the
lower and upper regions
of the body.
But the lotuses
open and shut
as the sun
in the body
rises and sets.

On which of these blooms
is the full moon born,
and on which the darkest
night of the month?

On which of these lotuses
rests the total eclipse
of the sun
and the moon?

           ✎ Chandidās Gosāiñ

---

[1]These verses refer to the yogic interpretation of psychic energy
that is said to be carried by *sushumnā*, the symbolic central vein
that runs along the spinal column. There are six *chakras* (wheels)
placed at different points on the *sushumnā* for relaying the
psychic energy. The *chakras* are visual images of lotuses with
varying numbers of petals. According to the Bāul concept,

The Master of the universe
belongs to no one
but you must find him.
As you explore your mind
looking for him,
feelings override thoughts.

Appearing, vanishing,
again and again,
breathing life into life,
he who is life
eats of its hidden riches.

Chandidās Gosāiñ

mūlādhāra, which is the lowest *chakra*, placed behind the genitals, is referred to as a lotus of four petals, and *sahasrāra*, at the top end of the vein *sushumnā*, blossoming inside the skull, is assessed to be a lotus of a thousand petals. See also notes on *Vishuddha-chakra* (p. 107) *Mūlādhāra-chakra* (p. 108) and *Dvidal-chakra* (p. 147).

My worries continue
for my crumbling boat[1]
can no longer carry—
water rushes through her hulk
and salt eats at her keel.
My boat can bear no more
the burden of water.

O Master of my life,
open your eyes,
show me your kindness
and hold me as I die.
I can never be
as I am again.

There lay the river Hooghly
as I moored my boat.
Reaching the jetty at Kālnā,
I cast the anchor deep.
Passions like bandits
leapt at me,
raided my boat,
and went off with the spoils.
They cut the mooring rope
and left me adrift.

[1]River, symbol for life; boat, symbol for the human body.

The Master says:
wash away
the stains of your heart,
then your boat will carry
tranquility.

ఇ *Chiru*

My unknowing heart,
can you not lay the snare
that catches the moon?[1]

Your eyes are dilated
by your ceaseless effort
as you try to sieze
the sky at one single leap.

ఇ *Dīn*

[1]*Chandra*, *chānd* and *Krishnachandra*—the moon and the black
moon—represent Krishna, God.

You are free to act
as you wish.
I measure your acts.

            ❧ *Dwija Āshutosh*

If love's green foliage
can destroy your balance,
when facing the roots
you will be as a stranger,
lost.

            ❧ *Dwija Gadādhar*

Never plunge
into the river of lust,
you will not reach the bank.
It is a boundless river
where typhoons rage.

            ❧ *Dwija Kailāshchandra*

Go to the home
of beauty and form
should you wish to see
the man within.

His ways cross
the sphere
where life lives with death
and sense with insanity.
Close your eyes
and try to catch him.
He is slipping by.

∾ Erfān Shāh

To find nectar
stir the cauldron
on the fire—
and unite the act of loving
with the feeling for love.

Distill the sweetness
of the heart
and reach the treasures,
devoting yourself
to those wholly devoted.

Sweetness rests
in the moon
and nectar
in the flowers.

Erfān Shāh

My soul cries out,
snared by the beauty
of the formless one.
As I cry by myself,
night and day,
beauty amassed before my eyes
surpasses numberless moons and suns.
If I look at the clouds in the sky,
I see his beauty afloat;
and I see him walk on the stars
blazing my heart.

✌ Fikirchānd[1]

---

[1]*Chandra, chānd* and *Krishnachandra*—the moon and the black moon—represent Krishna, God.

The eyes see
and the skin feels
the dust and the dirt.
Tasted on the tongue of life,
the lord of love is true.
Flowers of form
and the flavors of love
blossom and wilt,
but where lies the thread of feeling?

My lord is playing his flute
out of doors
as I restlessly ache
listening to him.
I could not gather
the garland of greeting
and in shame I go my way—
further and further,
yet I still hear the tune.

What good is distance for a serving soul?
The world is a city of my lord.
He is the sea and the river
as well as the keeper
of the landing-stage.

Gangārām

My life is a little oil lamp
floating on the waves.
But from which landing-pier
did you set me afloat?
With darkness ahead of me
and darkness behind,
darkness overlaps my night,
while the necklace of waves
constantly rings me about.
The storm of the night
relentlessly flows
below the stars,
and the lamp is afloat
on the shoreless water—
for company.

      Gangārām

As the dumb one sings
for the deaf,
the handless plays the lute
and the cripple leads the dance.
The blind watch,
engrossed in the show.
What a strange world is this!

      Gaurchānd

What is the use of calling someone who
    does not respond?
What evidence do I have that he can hear
    my heart?
No one can describe his shape or his
    complexion,
yet everyone is busy talking about him,
making special announcements.
I laugh as I listen.
I have never seen him since my birth.
How do I know whether he exists or not?
As I see it,
they all appear to grope in darkness, trying
    to reach him.

Some say he lives in heaven,
others, that his home is not to be known.
I hear them,
but every single statement leaves me more
    and more confused.
Hoping to find him, some pray;
some go on pilgrimage, and others fast.
Some become vegetarians,
others wear the ochre robe.

The Mussulmans call him Allah
and the Christians, Jesus Christ.
The Hindus call him Bhagavān.
I have no doubt they are one.
Judging all the points,
I feel that God exists on his own,
immensely, immeasurably,
but adorned with shapes.
The ocean or a drop of water, each is God;
each of them shines with its own brilliance
within God.

≈ Gobinda Dās

I often repeat the word "I," but who is the I
    within myself?
I am not sure.
My I eats no rice or vegetables, savories or
    sweets,
butter or cheese.
Expensive shawls are not for that I.
Colorful jackets or shirts are useless.
Even a scrap of loin-cloth is not needed.
This I has no status or profession.
It is not a lawyer or an advocate, a district
    magistrate
or a porter, a handyman or a servant.
It is neither a sage nor a monk,
neither a householder not an ascetic living in
    the forest.
This I has no desire
for the day-to-day ritual of righteous
    living.
As I is the very basis of spirituality,
worship, prayers or meditations are superfluous
    for it.
This I is not locked into one dwelling:
its relationship with the body
resembles that of the bird with the tree.
The bird lives on the tree but does not grow
    on it.

The I is not concerned with love or hate,
and yet it is intimate with all beings.
This I is like a conjuror,
able to assume a multitude of characters in
    many garments.
But when removed from one, it returns to its
    origin.
And there, it needs no name
such as Gaur, Gadāi or Gopikānta, Keshab or
    Kenārām;
or surnames or titles.
It has no trace of caste, class or race.

        Gobne Dās
        (possibly *Gobinda Dās)*

Judge your public
then choose your words.
If you speak the truth
you will be struck by a stick.
If you lie
you will charm the world.

        Gobinda Dās

That enchanting river
reflects the very form
of the formless one.
Sense the essence of the matter,
my undiscerning heart,
and feel the taste
on your tongue.

You see only
a little ditch of life
and remain lying in it
in a drunken stupor.

        ~ *Gopāl*

The leaves are bejewelled
by the moon,[1]
as you can see,
but where, my heart,
are the roots
of the plant?

On which water
floats the lotus bloom
where sits your teacher?
Gazelles leap about the lotus pond
and the black bee stings the bloom.

        ~ *Gopāl*

God has reversed the acts
of the play:
The land talks in paradox
and the flowers devour
the heads of fruits,
and the gentle vine,
roaring,
strangles the tree.
The moon rises in the day
and the sun at night
with shining rays.

Blood is white,
and on a lake of blood
float a pair of swans
copulating continuously
in a jungle of lust and love.

        Gopāl

---

[1]*Chandra, chānd* and *Krishnachandra*—the moon and the black
moon—represent Krishna, God.

Sown on a slab of stone,
the seed of faith[1]
dries day by day
never sprouting.
You may cultivate
the arid earth
but the hardened seed
will yield no harvest.

Great is the woodland
where sandal grows,
the breeze,
bearing the scent of sandal,
perfumes the neighboring trees,
turning them into sandalwood.

Gosāiñ Charan

Do not forget
that your body contains
the whole of existence.

Gosāiñ Gopāl

[1]*Bijamantra*: see note 2, p. 61.

The man who breathes
lives on air
and the other, unseen,
lies beyond reach.
Between the two
moves another man
as a secret link.
Worship knowingly.
There is sport
amongst the three of them.

My searching heart,
whom do you seek?

Between the doors
of birth and death
stands yet another door,
wholly inexplicable.
He who is able
to be born
at the door of death
is devoted eternally.

Die before dying,
die living.

                Gosāiñ Gopāl

When the confluence
of the three rivers[1]
dries out,
and the great fish,[2]
preserver-Vishnu's
first expression of life,
vanishes away,
death's god detains you.
Wild illusions
confuse your path to reality
making you forget
what the teacher had taught you.
Day by day
your life slips by in lethargy.

If you wish to hold the moon in your hands,
clip the noose
around your neck
and worship love.

[1]The confluence of the Ganges, the Jamunā, and the Saraswati at
Prayag, near Allahabad in north India. Called *Tribeni*, the Bāuls
use the term in a metaphysical sense, implying the meeting
ground of body, mind, and spirit; of heaven, earth, and the nether
world; of desire, love, and devotion to God.
[2]*Min*, the first reincarnation, in the form of a fish, of Vishnu, the
preserving power of the Hindu triple forces.

The teacher is the fish,[3]
the first to find life
in the turbulent junction
of the three rivers—
high waves billowing.
If you wish to meet
the great fish of life
be aware.
Careless,
you will encounter death.

Shut doors
on the face of lust.
Attain the greatest
—the unattainable man—[4]
and act as lovers act.
Meet death before you die.

✦ Gosāiñ Gopāl

[3]*Min*: see note 2.
[4]God, unattainable by the senses, formless.

Where is the home
of the moon?
And what makes
the cycle of the days
wander encircling
the moving nights?

The lunar eclipse
on the night of the full moon
is known to all.
But no one enquires
about the blackened moon
on the darkest night
of the month.

He who is able to make
the full moon rise
in the sky
of the darkest night
has a right to claim
the glory of the three worlds:
heaven, earth, and the nether spheres.

Gosāiñ Gopāl

Reaching for reality
is lame talk
to describe the goal
of the lover-worshipper.

He will attain
the great unattainable,
and stare at the face
of the invisible one,
bearing the nectar of love.

          Gosāiñ Gopāl

Unaware of its essential spirit,
when you fall in love
you commit human sacrifice
at the river bank of feelings.

          Gosāiñ Phatik
          (Phatik Chānd)

The rites of violent love
rest in the essence
of supreme beauty
and in the dignity of *yoga*[1]
as the adept knows.

Awarding his hands
to the fangs of a snake,
fearless, he lives.
The poison and ambrosia
of immortal life
are one and the same to him.
He is dead
while wholly living.

The essence of beauty
in the mirror of love
stares at his face:
the formless
within the visible form.
The fire cools
in his hands
and quicksilver roasts
on the flames.

ও Guruchānd

[1]*Yoga*, union, the path to the unity of body, mind, and spirit
through physical and mental discipline.

I am forbidden to reveal
the secret of my heart
but my life falters
seeking total absorption.
Danger threatens
if I fail to know
the nature of the heart
that shares my pain.

Love springs
and feelings merge.
Divided forms unite.
A pair of hearts
flowing in twin streams
long to reach the god of love.

Haridās

Those who are dead
and yet fully alive
and know the flavors of feelings
in loving,
they will cross the river.
Gazing at the stream of life
and death,
they seek integrity.
They have no wish
for happiness,
walking against the wind.

They kill lust
with lust,
and enter the city of love
unattached.

Haridās

Will the day ever dawn
when the treasured man[1] of my heart
will become my own?
Though not cast in any shape,
he is seen
in the ways of love.

Those who are absorbed
by the flavors of feelings
and are wholly living
with the knowledge of death
have defeated their foes—
pride, envy, lust and anger,
ignorance and greed.

If your life, flowing with life,
longs for the man,
he will come
with kindly steps.
Look in the worlds
of god, demon, and man;[2]
he is already there.

        Haridās

---

[1]God, unattainable by the senses, formless.
[2]*Triloka: Svarga, martya,* and *pātāla,* the three worlds—heaven, earth, and the nether-world—which are inhabited by Gods, men, and demons, respectively.

Free impulses
live together
with the forces of abstinence.
Feminine energy entwined
with the spirit of man
resemble the tuned strings
of the lute,
wholly indivisible.
The heart is the home
where there is
no separation.

Hāude Gosāiñ

He who knows
the essence of love
fears none.
Devoted only to
love's own form
alive before his eyes,
his home is in
happiness itself.

Lulling lust
by lust alone,
he raises the heart
of the god that churns all hearts,[1]
finding himself
in perennial love.

❧ Hāude Gosāiñ

---

[1] *Manmatha* (mind-churner): the God of love.

The energy of impulse
must burn itself out
on a heap of glowing jewels.
He who lives
must die
to fulfill the world of cause.

ॐ Hāude Gosāiñ

When life, mind, and sight
are in agreement
the target is
within your reach:
you can see
the formless *Brahma*
with bare eyes.

ॐ Hāude Gosāiñ

How can you walk
the ways of love
carrying stolen loot
with impunity?

In the forest of Brindā[1]
loving is worshipping.
The riches raised from rubbish
are measured with care
in a jeweller's balance.
The land is ruled by women
with lovers as their vassals.
The greedy and lusting thieves
are outlawed, enchained.

As the essence of purity[2]
in the brilliance of the sky,
love transcends lust
evolving ecstasy.
The bellows breathe
into the fire of life
and stabilize mercury.

        Hāude Gosāiñ

---

[1]Brindāban, a town in north India where Krishna spent his days as a youth.

[2]*Vishuddha-chakra*, one of the six symbolic lotuses representing stages in the spiritual body of man, is related to the throat; has sixteen petals, is smoke-grey, and represents purity. See also note on lotus blooms (p. 79).

On the other shore
of the ocean
of one's own self
quivers a drop of fluid,
the origin of all.
But who can cross the seas
to reach it.

The root of all[1]
is planted in you.
Explore the ground
to reach the essence.

           ✍ *Hāude Gosāiñ*

[1]*Mūlādhāra-chakra.* The first of the six stages of man's spiritual body, represented by a lotus of four petals, is related to the area between the anus and the genital organ, is red, and represents respiration and life in yogic terms. See also note on lotus blooms (p. 79).

Release the sensation of taste
on your tongue.
Open the doors of feeling
for beloved Krishna,
the image of eternal love.
Nectar, showering
on the lotus of spontaneity,
runs down the stem
to be one with the water
where flowers lie.

Lust and love
and the erotic acts
are housed in one single place
where sorrows and joys
do not exist.

Hāude Gosāiñ

Worship God if you wish,
but skip the fancy-dress
and the silly pose . . .

Hāude Gosāiñ

That boat, like a racer,
flies in the air;
mine is a dinghy,[1]
old and rotten,
dragging in the water
the whole night long
while I bale out the water.
Old is my boat,
crumbling to pieces.
The mast is useless.
How can I sail
my rotten old boat
as the storm
rages round me?

        Ishān Jugi

[1]River, symbol for life; boat, symbol for the human body.

Light has burst
on the walls of the sky,
the kind one has blossomed at last.
Waking in the morning
I saw him present,
appearing close to my face.

Flowers wither and birds flutter,
the dew forms on the leaves.
The glow of the night is melting away
with the rising heat of the sun.
The kind one is the light of the moon.

Ishān cries as he ponders these things
with a sense of deep pain.

∽ Ishān Jugi

My lord is not a broken wheel
that groans as it turns.
Tell me, my silent Master,
O my lord,
what worship may open me
to *Brahma's* lotus bloom?

The stars and the moon eternally move
making no sound.
Each cycle of the universe
in silence prays,
welling up with the essence of love.

Ishān Jugi

My heart is saturated
but with what?
Joy or death?
What good is there in calling God
as I no longer lean
on the future or past?
My heart dances with unique joy,
for his anklet-bells
jingle night and day.

A sense of wonder has overtaken all:
where is that ocean
and where are the rivers?
And yet the waves are there
for you to observe
only if you unite your eyes
with your heart.

If you wish to view such spectacular play
mingle your heart
with the eyes of your heart.

Ishān Jugi

I am fulfilled
being the breath you blow
on your flute.
I am not sad
if I end with one single tune.
Your flute is the universe
of three different worlds
of god, demon, and man,[1]
I am the breath you blow.

Tuned to your finger-holes,
right or wrong,
I sound through sleepless nights.
I sound through the months
of monsoon and spring
bound with your heart.

I feel no sadness at complete dissolution.
What more could I wish
than to dissolve
in the breath of your melody?

        Ishān Jugi

---

[1]*Triloka*: see note 2, p. 103.

How can I capture the man[1]
who is not to be caught?
He lives on the other bank
of the river.[2]
The membrane of my eyes
screens my vision.

         ☙ *Jādubindu*

Blind one,
how can you stumble
on a straight
and inborn path?[3]
Be natural
with your self,
and find the way
that is within you.

         ☙ *Jādubindu*

---

[1]God, unattainable by the senses, formless.
[2]The river Birajā. Birajā was one of the secret loves of Krishna. When Rādhā came to know about this affair, Birajā, abandoning life, changed into a river. The Bāuls consider the other bank of the river Birajā as heaven.
[3]*Sahaja*, inborn, spontaneous. The *sahaja* path represents a religious movement within the fold of Vaishnavism. See Deben Bhattacharya, *Love Songs of Chandidās*, George Allen & Unwin, London, 1967.

115

Pour out the cloudy fluid,
O angry tapper.
Hacking instead of tapping
at a date-palm tree
is useless.

The tapper of love
works his way up
to the top
aided by the mind;
the supporting strap
tied in a loop
around the tree.

Piercing the heart
with a sharp-edged knife,
he opens the course
for torrents of
sweet, crystalline juice.

Jādubindu

I plunged into the water
like a fisherman,
hoping to catch
the fish of faith.
Devotion,
which was my fishing net,
was torn to pieces.
I only gathered
some useless shells—
jealousy and blame—
churning the mud
in vain.

❧ Jādubindu

Look, look for him[1]
in the temple of your limbs.
He is there
as the lord of the world,
speaking,
singing
in enchanting tunes.
He is an expert
at hide-and-seek,
no one can see him.
He is the universe
with no form of his own.

Do not try to catch him,
O my heart,
he can never be caught.
You can only hope for him
in faith,
in complete faith.

Jādubindu

---

[1]God, unattainable by the senses, formless.

The perilous confluence
of the three rivers,
penetrates the nether-world,
causing instant death
if you step into it.
In a raging typhoon,
the tidal waves
and the ebbing water
flow concurrently,
night and day.

You cannot row a boat[2]
on this shoreless ocean.
Saints are dying in it
and the gods are drowning.

Speechlessly,
sages and seekers gaze
at the river-line
as it bends away
with the horizon.

❧ Jādubindu

---

[1]*Tribeni*: see note 1, p. 96.
[2]River, symbol for life; boat, symbol for the human body.

Plowman
are you out of your wits
not to take care
of your own land?

A squadron of six birds[1]
is picking at the rice,
grown golden and ripe
in the field of your limbs.

Farming the splendid
measured land
of this human body,
you raised the crop
of devotion to God.
But passions eat it
like sparrows.

The fence of consciousness
lies in the dust,
leaving gaps for
cattle to clamber through
to feast on your harvest.

~ *Jādubindu*[2]

---

[1]The six enemies or weaknesses of man *(shadaripu)*: lust, anger, greed, ignorance, pride, and envy.
[2]Tape-recorded in Siuri, Birbhum, in 1954. Singer: Purna Chandra, son of Nabanidās Bāul.

Shame on you
my shameless heart—
what now can I say?

You have gathered a piece of glass
at the price of gold.
In spite of a pair of eyes,
you missed the valuable jewels,
caring only for worthless stones.
Wandering blindly,
you could not see
that the house overflowed
with the choicest rubies
and diamonds
and gems of fire.

Hugging a sickle
in your waistband,
what do you search
from field to field?
What is the use?

My heart,
will you not explore for once
the home of beauty?

                            ✋ *Jādubindu*

On the dangerous currents
of the river of life,
wicked is the oarsman
of my heart:
having eaten the whole fare,
he refuses to row.

        Jaladhar

If you fail to recognize
your own heart,
can you ever come to know
the great unknown?

The farthest away
will be nearest to you,
and the unknown
within your knowing.

Fill up your home
with the world,
and you will attain
the unattainable man.[1]

        Kālāchānd

[1]God, unattainable by the senses, formless.

The body of man
is a land for wish-fulfillment:
care will produce
a harvest of jewels.
Plow it at a propitious time.
Hopes that ushered you
into this material world
will bear fruit.

Action is the steel
for your plow,
passions are oxen.
Sow your seeds on ready land;
treasures will be yours
at harvest time.

The seed rests
in the root of the tree.

        ∾ Kālāchānd

Have faith.
Fate achieves nothing.
In faith rests
the most valuable wealth.

        ∾ Kālāchānd

The primeval man,[1]
called the imperishable,
is eternally aloft.
His form,
as subtle as infinity,
roams emptiness,
the universe of nothing.

His will produced
one primal drop,[2]
which bore the seed
and the flower
and the fruit—
all in the nature
of one single drop.

❧ Kālāchānd

[1]God, unattainable by the senses, formless.
[2]*Bindu*, the cosmic drop; the point of emergence and dissolution representing the whole; the immense contained in the minute.

124

Gay and glorious
to the eyes,
the flower opens
in a world of colors
and yet remains unshaped.

Poison encircles the bloom
but the devout eats the venom
and digests it.
The flower opens to be seen
all the year round.

                                Kānāi

Let your heart be a caring home
for the man of your heart.[1]

Focus your vision
through the eye-black
of loving,
he will be floating
on the mercurial mirror.

Hours wither
like broken games
on the playground of the earth.
Abandon the search
and join the game of love.

          ✌ *Kānāilāl*

Poison that kills a man
can also cure
depending on the physician's skill.
"That which gives life gives death"
is the maxim
for worshipping God.

          ✌ *Krishnadās*

[1]God, unattainable by the senses, formless.

Those who judge by caste
practice evil,
they find nothing.
God is reached when caste has vanished.
How can I boast of my caste
if it spurns friendship?
I could light a fire
and burn it.

       Lālan

Formless,
the flower floats.
But where is the plant
and the water?
Yet still the flower
eternally floats
on the waves of life.
The droning bees
drink its honey
while Lālan,
seeking, chasing,
misses the flower.

       Lālan

What blame may I heap
on my chosen scapegoat?
My nature is at fault
causing confusion.

The hopes that brought me into
this world
ruthlessly smashed the home of my hope,
my fate is in a state of ruin.
I made a monkey
out of God.

≈ *Lālan*

And as yet
the heart of my heart
knows no better:
where am I
and where shall I be,
and when,
with whom?

The futile words
"my house, my home"
are razed to the dust
as the eyelids blink.

While dreams add
to the bricks
of my mansions,
my foolish heart
marches to its funeral
without even knowing it.

෴ *Lālan*

Never in my life
did I once face
the man who lives
in my own little room.[1]

My eyes, blinded
by the weight of storms,
can see nothing,
even when he stirs.
My hands
fail to reach him
as they are forever engaged
with the world.

I keep silent
when they call him
the bird of life
and of water
and of fire
and earth
and air—
while no one is sure.

Could I ever wish
to know anyone else?
I do not yet know
my own little room.

            ❧ *Lālan*

[1]The body.

Silence makes its nest
in the midst of uproar.

❧ Lālan

A thief in my own home,
I chain my hands and feet
to punish myself.
I do not discuss
my helpless state.
I keep quiet.

❧ Lālan

No words can describe
the rain-bird's[1] love
for the cloud
and its water.

Clouds deceive it
and yet flies the bird
eager to drink,
gazing, gazing at the clouds,
never blinking.

The way of all rain-birds
is death from thirst.
They will not drink
unless the clouds break.

Lālan

[1]*Chātaka*: see note 1, p. 64.

Watch out for blunders,
my heart,
when engaged with this world.
You chose to renounce it,
yet fly your loin-cloth
as a glorious flag.

Act as you must,
my heart,
but remember,
your past goes with you.

           Lālan

This land offered me
only dubious joys.
Where else could I go?

I found a broken boat[1]
and spent my life
bailing out the water.

           Lālan

[1]River, symbol for life; boat, symbol for the human body.

I have no knowledge
of my self.
If for once I could know
what I am,
the unknown would be known.

God is near
and yet far away,
like the mountain hiding
behind my screening hair.
I travel to the distant towns
of Dhaka and Delhi,
constantly searching.
But I am only
circling around my knees.

God is alive
in my living room.
Only purity of heart
will lead me to him.
The more I study
the wisdom of the *Vedas*[1]
the more I am bewildered,
repeating "I."
O my heart,
seek shelter at his feet,
he who knows the word "I."

Lālan says
with a confused heart:
I am blind
in spite of my eyes.

        ❧ *Lālan*[2]

My heart is not
to my heart's liking.
I wish I knew
how to unite the two.

        ❧ *Lālan*

[1]The *Vedas*: see note 1, p. 43.
[2]Tape-recorded in Calcutta, in 1954. Singer: Bhaktadās Bāul. See record No. BAM-LD 099, *Religious Songs from Bengal*, Paris, 1966.

Can I ever again be born as a man?
Hurry up, my heart,[1]
and act as you wish
in this world.

God has created man
in immortal form,
wishing to be human.
Nothing is better than man.

Great is your luck,
my heart,
to become the boat
of human life.

Follow the current
and set sail.
Do not sink the boat
that carries you.

The human shape
is made by God
since man can pray
only by loving.[2]

[1]*Mon*: see note 2, p. 47.
[2]*Mādhurya*, represents the gentle and loving aspect of God
according to Vaishnava classification.

Do not miss the shores
nor lose the sail.

     ❧ *Lālan*

I wish to go to Kāshi.[1]
The noose of *karma*,[2]
closing round my neck,
makes me move
as in a carousel.
My foolish heart
brought me to this state
of near disaster.
My boat will certainly sink
in the narrow waterways
of being born
and born again.

     ❧ *Lālan*

---

[1]Kāshi, Vārānasi, or Benares, on the banks of the Ganges, is one of the most sacred places of Hindu pilgrimage in north India.
[2]*Karma*, one's actions, work, or deeds, the effect of which continues after death in the process of reincarnation.

How long shall it be
before I can see the moon,[1]
removing the darkness
of my heart?

That kind moon
who brought me to this world,
what prayers may I offer to him
and what meditations?

Shall I go to Kāshi[2]
on a pilgrimage
or stay in a forest?
O where shall I go
to find my moon?

❧ Lālan

[1]*Chandra, chānd* and *Krishnachandra*—the moon and the black
moon—represents Krishna, God.
[2]Kāshi: see note 1, p. 137.

My heart,
you are in a muddle.
As the days go by,
your inherited riches
plundered, fly.
You only doze
around the clock
drinking dreams[1]
and living in five homes[2]
with no control.

The robber rests with you,
my heart,
in your own room.[3]
But how can you know?
Your eyes are shut
in sleep.

≈ *Lālan*

[1]Illusions.
[2]The five elements: earth, water, fire, air, and ether.
[3]The body.

Please, Kānāi,[1]
come to Braja[2] for once
to see the state of the land
and how your mother, Jashodā, fares.
Father Nanda, pained at your parting,
is blinded by tears,
and your cowherd friends
and thrown into confusion.

The young and the aged
are joyless
constantly longing to be at your precious
    feet.
The animals and the birds
are restless, fitful,
not hearing your flute sing.

∼ *Lālan*

---

[1]A diminutive term for Krishna.
[2]Braja is the name of the region in north India that includes
Mathura, Brindaban, Gokul, Govardhan, and the surrounding area
where Krishna spent his days in youth.

What is the color of your love,
O my insane heart,
that you wish to renounce the world
as an ascetic for Islam?

The Hindus and Muslims
are sundered in two.
The Muslims aspire
to their particular heaven
named *Behest*,
and the Hindus to theirs
called *Svarga*.
Both words,
like formal gates,
are lifeless.
Who cares for them?

              ❧ *Lālan*

Do not count on your breath,
it will let you down
as fast as an eyelid falls.
Hopes that you nestled
will be buried with your heart.
If you wish to achieve
act while you breathe.

              ❧ *Lālan*

Poison and nectar
are mingled in one,
like music
played and heard
in a single act.

The human heart,
free from flaw,
forever enlightened,
sees good and evil
sharing the same
time and place.

A child sucking at the breast
of his mother
draws milk.
A leech at the breast
of a woman
draws blood.

          Lālan

Who can you call your own,
my heart?
For whom do you shed
your futile tears?

Brothers and friends—
let them be;
the world is there.
Your own dear life
is hardly your own.

You have come alone,
you will go alone.

✍ Lālan

143

Bāul Torap Shah, from Jessore, Bangladesh
(with swarāj*).*

A man unknown to me
and I,
we live together
but in a void,
a million miles
between us.

My eyes blindfolded
by worldly dreams
cannot recognize him,
or understand.

               ❧ *Lālan*

The scriptures will teach you
no prayers for love.
Love's records remain
unsigned by sages.

               ❧ *Lālan*

He talks to me
but he does not let me see him.
He moves
close to my hands
but away from my reach.
I explore
the sky and the earth
searching for him,
circling round my error
of not knowing my self.
Who am I
and who is he?

Lālan[1]

---

[1]Tape-recorded in Calcutta, 1971. Singer: Bāul Torap Shah, from Jessore, Bangladesh.

As the man and the woman in me
unite in love,
the brilliant beauty
balanced on the two-petalled lotus[1]
within me
dazzles my eyes.
The rays
outshine the moon
and the jewels
glowing on the hoods of snakes.[2]

My skin and bone
are turned to gold.
I am the reservoir of love
alive as the waves.
A single drop of water
has grown into a sea,
unnavigable.

     Lālan

---

[1]*Dvidal-chakra* (or, *ājnā-chakra*), one of the six stages of man's
spiritual body, represented by a lotus of two petals, related to the
area between the eyebrows, is white, and represents male and
female elements in a united form. Also see note on lotus blooms
(pp. 78-79).
[2]According to Bengali legends, the most precious jewel in the
world is found on the hoods of certain poisonous snakes.

The moon is encircled by moons.[1]
How can I hold it
in my hands?
The unseizable moon,[2]
glowing in the brilliance
of a million moons,
rocks my head
in a lunar carnival.

Fruits adorn
the tree of the moon,
flashing,
luminously flashing.
I try to look
but my eyes cannot bear
the power
of that radiant beauty.

          Lālan

[1]This song appears similar to Vaishnava poems expressing
Rādhā's and Krishna's dazzling beauty.
[2]God, unattainable by the senses, formless.

Pandemonium broke loose
in the guard-room of love.
My heart was caught
like a thief
by the greatest of lovers[1]
who had set snares
in the air.

❧ *Lālan*

The day I become a resident
of the cremation ground
what riches will I carry
but a ghost's load?

❧ *Lālan*

---

[1]*Rasik*, an adept in the knowledge of the essence of feelings; as
an adjective, often attributed to Krishna.

The key to my home
is in alien hands.
How can I enter
to gaze at my riches?

My home is loaded with gold
but run by a stranger
who is blind from birth.
He would let me in
if I paid my entrance fees.

As I do not know
who he is
I wander the streets
of error.

Lālan

Could I ever forget him
since I delivered my heart
at his feet?
His beauty enchants my eyes
wherever I steer myself
around the compass.

Though all call him black[1]
he is not that,
he is the glow of the moon,
the black moon,
and there is no other moon
to equal him.

        Lālan

---

[1]*Chandra, chānd* and *Krishnachandra*—the moon and the black moon—represent Krishna, God.

Sixteen gangsters[1]
of the city
are running loose,
looting all.
The five wealthy ones[2]
are nearly lost;
trade is at
the breaking point.

The king of kings
is also king of the thieves.
To whom may I complain?

The riches, all are gone
leaving only an empty room[3]
to my credit.

Says Lālan:
the room will pay
for tax claims.

       ❧ Lālan

---

[1]*Jnānendriya*, the five forces of perception: ears, skin, eyes, nose, and tongue for tasting; *karmendriya*, the five forces of action: anus, genital organ, hands, feet, and tongue for speaking; and *shadaripu*, the six inimical forces: lust, anger, greed, ignorance, pride, and envy.
[2]Conscience, wisdom, restraint, renunciation, and devotion.
[3]The body.

I am afraid
of the divine sport:
the boat carrying the river[1]
marching on the land.

This is the nature
of the Ganges of life.
Rising with the rains
it dries again
at an eyelid's wink.

Flowers blossom
adorning its waters.
Fruits form unseen.
And pervading all,
the fish, the preserver of life[2]
playfully floats
in the river.

Says Lālan:
the fish too will go
when the river evaporates.

Lālan

[1]River, symbol for life; boat, symbol for the human body.
[2]*Min*: see note 2, p. 96.

Search the banks
of the river of being
to find divine riches.
Its water shines
with the lustre of pearls.
Islands rise
at an eyelid's blink
where sages may live.
Fishing that river
is no easy task:
waves billow
though there is no wind.
But lovers dive
to raise treasures.

Lālan

Frightened since birth,
you kept away from the path of life.
You achieved nothing.

Lālan

How the days drag
before my union
with the man of my heart!
Round the hours
of the day and night
as the rain-bird[1]
watches the clouds,
I gaze at the black moon[2]
hoping to surrender myself
at his feet,
but in vain.

Like lightning,
flickering through the clouds
then hiding
never to be found again,
I saw his beauty
flashing through my dream
and I lost Krishna.

      Lālan

[1]*Chātaka:* see note 1, p. 64.
[2]*Chandra, chānd* and *Krishnachandra*—the moon and the black moon—represent Krishna, God.

The road to you is blocked
by temples and mosques.
I hear your call, my Lord,
but I cannot advance,
prophets and teachers
bar my way.

Since I would wish
to burn the world
with that which cools my limbs,
my devotion to unity
dies divided.

The doors of love bear many locks;
scriptures and beads.

Madan, in tears,
dies of regret and pain.

         Madan

The sea of life is full of treasures:
the diver finds pearls
and the fisherman fish.

         Madan

Even if you forbid,
dear friend,
I am helpless;
my songs contain
my prayers.

Some flowers pray
through the radiance
of their colors
and others, being dark,
with fragrance.
As the *vinā* prays
with its vibrating strings,
do I with my songs.

⤙ *Madan*

The subterranean stream
flowing through the heart of the earth
is constantly present
and yet, invisible.

God reminds me
of this undefined river,
and I am afraid of
discussing him.

⤙ *Madan*

O cruelly eager one,
are you going to destroy in fire
your heart's flower-bud?
Would you force it to blossom,
let the fragrance escape,
not biding your time?

Look at my master, God,
eternally opening the buds in bloom
but never in a hurry.
You are dependent
on the hours of the day
because of your terrifying greed.
What else can you do?

Listen to Madan's appeal
and do not hurt the Master at heart:
the stream spontaneously flows
lost in itself,
listening to his words,
O eager one.

Madan

I shall not open my eyes again
if I do not see him at first sight.
Can you then tell me
through the sense of smell
and through my listening ears
that he has come?
That he has come
to the sky in the east,
that your friend has come
to the sky of the east.

Did the lotus open its eyes
and I did not see?
But the crimson glow of the rising sun
rocked it to sleep
on the mattress of night.
I shall not open my eyes again
if I do not see him at first sight.

Madan

The so-called lovers
rarely know
the essence of loving.
A lover lives
for love alone
as the fish in the water.

Great is the lover
who can love day and night,
and is wholly devoted
to love's intercourse:
worship with prayer.

The man or the woman
remains alone,
but a lover is formed
when souls conjoin.

Manohar

All can see
when a forest is on fire,
but none can trace
the fire of my heart.

Miyājān Fakir

Your heart
is a piece of paper.
The figures
you have written there
cannot be known
except by the heart.

          Narahari

Hopes filled my heart
that trade would double.
But fire entered
the nest of my hope
burning it to ashes:
ships loaded with merchandise
went down in a typhoon.

          Narahari Gosāin

Religion rests
in each one's consciousness;
a private path.
He who is devoted
can abandon all.

          Narahari Gosāin

A lover who labors
to find the essence of love
earns wages
four times his worth,
and an old age pension on top.

      ∾ *Narahari Gosāin*

The act of loving
is not an idle dream.
Loving grows
from the grilling of lust,
like feeling death,
being wholly alive.

The clay beetle
buried in the earth
lives on clay,
nestling in it.

Lovers know how love
can overcome lust,
though an uphill walk
even for a man of strength.

      ∾ *Nārān*

Groping for the river,[1]
O my senseless heart,
in vain do you wander
from place to place.
The ocean of your heart
bears a priceless gem.
What good is life
if you fail to find
the spontaneous man[2]
who dwells in your body?
Your destiny is shamed.

Do not give up gold
for a piece of glass,
nor leave the way to heaven
for a visit to hell.
What good is there
in wandering round the world?
The infinite resides
in your own little room.[3]

       Nitāidās

[1]River, symbol for life; boat, symbol for the human body.
[2]*Sahaja*: see note 3, p. 115.
[3]The body.

Plunging deep into the sea
of beauty,
some swim
and others sink.

The jewel set in the hood
of a snake[1]
enriches the man
who can tame the beast.
Those unaware of the flavors of feeling
are bitten to death.

The jewel resting
at the bottom of the sea
is gathered by the diver
to enhance his life.
Those unable to dive to that depth
choke and die.

Lust mingles with love
like water with milk.
An adept, as pure as the swan,
is able to distill it.

Nitya Khyepā

[1]According to Bengali legends, the most precious jewel in the world is found on the hoods of certain poisonous snakes.

Why do you fail to visit
your own soul
while wandering in vain
round a pilgrim's course?

Nitāidās

Cry for the unknown
to know another heart.
Through the remote
find intimacy.

Gathering planks
and pieces of metal,
you build a boat
to float on the sea,
but those elements
are alien to water.

The boat sails
and then sinks,
but the tie of love
is never torn.

Nitya Khyepā

Brothers,
come along
if you wish to smoke
the hemp of love.
With mounting intoxication
dissolve the habits
of your settled home
and take shelter
in the lord of faith.

He who smokes
the hemp of love
is wholly unaffected
by the drug.

          Panchānan

How can the rays of the sun
conjugate with the lotus?
That is love,
not to be clouded by knowledge.

Keep your feet dry
as you walk by the sea.
Let attachments share the same home
but be unattached.

          Pāñchu

Strike your Master hard
and worship in faith.
If you wish to be devoted to God,
live unattached,
homeless,
in spite of a homestead
and your life with a girl.

Do not listen to your heart
that forever misleads.
Do not only think,
but chain your Master hand and foot.
Cut a cane of love
and flog him till he is blue.

The Master must eternally bow
at the feet of the disciple.

         ❧ *Pānchuchānd*

My heart is eaten away
by the white ants of the mind.

         ❧ *Pānja Shāh*

The shapes you have formed,
my lord,
like a potter,
vessel after vessel,
tell the tale of divine caprice
at the landing-stage of the river
and in the open field
and in the market place.

        Pānja Shāh

Life constrained by birth and death,
rests behind a bamboo screen
leaning on a stick.
Its thoughts filled
with useless junk,
it feeds on dust.

        Pānja Shāh

With a beggar's humility
I have come to your door,
O benign bearer of pain.[1]
No one is ever turned away
from your home of unending stores.
You have all the riches
in the worlds of god, demon, and man[2]
and so much have you given
without demand.

No more do I need any wealth,
O my Master.
Give me your feet.

          ∾ *Pānja Shāh*

Speak nothing
of the subtlety of love
to those unaware
of love's deeper sense.

You may keep in a cage
a parrot and a crow
and feed them with care
and teach them to sing.

The parrot will sing
but the crow will croak.

           Pānja Shāh

[1]God, unattainable by the senses, formless.
[2]*Triloka*: see note 2, p. 103.

What good is there
in being proud of one's race?
What can race do
either in this world or the other?
My heart bids me set funeral fires
to the face of race.

All my time passes,
being an honorable man,
bearing the burden of my race
and watching confusion.

People are chased from their lands
when the stomach hungers
and yet still they carry the load
of race:
Hindus and Mussulmans.
What is race and what are its signs?
You cannot eat it
nor can it cure an illness.

Pānja Shāh

That astounding flower
opening on the waters of the three streams[1]
enchants the worlds.

At times seen in flashes,
it hides below the waterline.

With no form of its own,
the eternal bloom
is the source of joy.

         ~ *Pānja Shāh*

If love should ever dawn
in your heart
fill your cup with arsenic.
It will turn to nectar,
giving life.

Soil erodes iron
but brings forth sweetness,
the nectar of fruit.

         ~ *Pānja Shāh*

[1]*Tribeni:* see note 1, p. 96.

He who has seen the beauty
of the beloved friend[1]
can never forget it.

It can be seen
but not discussed,
such beauty
has no comparison.

He who has seen that form
flashing in the mirror
loses the darkness of his heart.
He lives with his eyes
focused on that beauty,
careless of the river between life and death.

His heart forever devoted to beauty
dares the gods.

Pānja Shāh

[1] God, unattainable by the senses, formless.

Heaven does not lie
in the palm
of anyone's hand.
Do not dance for it.

            ❧ *Pānja Shāh*

When the clouds burst into blossom
the time will be propitious
for you to sit on the river bank
and contemplate.

You will see ten million places
where pilgrims gather,
and you will hold God
in the hollow of your hand.

            ❧ *Pānja Shāh*

Bāuls in their annual fair at Kenduli.

You cannot plow land
with a pair of oxen
of which one is fast
and the other slow.

᭡ *Paramānanda*

The pedantic scholar
is born blind:
he knows the scriptures
but misses the meaning.

᭡ *Paramānanda*

He who knows the ways
of the river of life
has no fear.
Rejecting safety at low tide,
he pulls the tow rope taut
on high tidal waves.

He bides his time by the river bank
when the tide engulfs the day.
At night when the moon ascends the sky
he ensnares its brilliance.

Wide and wild is the river of life
with splendid turbulence
where three streams meet.[1]
Each flows true to its course;
combined, they are a whirlpool.

He who can seize the vortex
of the confluence of the three streams
can swim with the joy of love.
He is not afraid of the hazard.

≈ *Phatik Chānd*

[1]*Tribeni*: see note 1, p. 96.

I wished to turn myself
into pure gold
by touching the philosopher's stone,
but I could not do it,
alas! I could not do it.

Impurity turned me
into an alloy.

        ❧ *Podo*

God has signalled
a new path.
Collect the holy books
and put them away.

        ❧ *Podo*

You have exposed yourself.
Blind,
in spite of your eyes,
you have offered your head
to a thief.
Soon it will fall.

        ❧ *Podo*

From the distance
of millions of miles
the sun's rays
open the petals
of the lotus.

But Podo is burnt to death
by the fire of feeling
in the midst of lotus blooms.

Life walks away
together with the days
and there are no songs
for God.

              Podo

The moon rises at high noon
and yet the night is long.

The darkest sky of the month
is alight with the full moon.
But the hours are still dark.

The sun has died
striking at our heart.

              Podo

My eyes are drowned by shadows,
the shades of feeling,
and the lotus of my heart
closes its petals
on the shore of darkness.
The Jamuna flows
dark and turbulent.

Floating on the water,
the flute of love
reaches my ears,
the flute of the lord of love.[1]
And I chase the world
as a Bāul would,
away from home, forgetting all.

I cry as I clutch the driftwood
on the waters of passion.
My eyes are drowned by shadows,
the shades of feeling.

Podo

[1]Krishna.

Not one single branch grows on that tree
yet new leaves shoot forth.
The tree encompasses the entire universe.

On top of it rests a flower, gently blossoming
as the bees hum around it.
So varied are the colors of the flower
that the world is utterly enchanted by it.

అ *Podo*

Having walked the pilgrim's path,
Podo plunged
into a green ditch of greed.
The sun scorched him,
fever seized him,
and now he is dying.

అ *Podo*

Do you wish to visit
my inner home
and drink nectar,
my heart?

Will you not enter
where lovers meet
in a joyous carnival,
singing of love?

Then walk the way
with a lamp of beauty,
leaving behind
this greed, that lust,
the ways of the world,
and all its qualities.[1]

Blame and violence,
old age and death,
dawn and dusk,
do not live there.
Only the radiance of color
brilliantly shines.

[1]The three *gunas*, or constituent qualities, which are inherent in
prakriti (the cosmic matter) are *sattva, rajas,* and *tamas. Sattva*
represents the virtue in truth and wisdom; *rajas,* action and
passion; and *tamas,* the dark forces of ignorance.

Songs of the Bauls of Bengal

There,
fire and explosives
are at home
together.

Podo

Will the man of love[1]
still wish to remain
in my broken-down home?
The spirit of my dwelling[2]
is in total disorder.

God brought us together,
like the hard-skinned coconut
with its thirst-quenching milk.
But how did the liquid
flow through that skin?
I would not know.

Like a dung beetle,
I was busy making a shell
for my own death.

Podo

[1]God, unattainable by the senses, formless.
[2]The body.

183

O my heart,[1]
come and mingle with my heart.
United,
let us visit the fantastic city.

Open the doors of love
to see the divine sport:
the boat floating
on dry land,
the frog singing of God.

Strange are the ways of that land.
Trees have no roots,
branches loaded with
the weight of feeling
rest in the sky,
flowering, fruiting.

There is not water there
nor any earth,
but the moat round the fort of the king
is overflowing with love.

≈ *Podo*

---

[1]*Mon*: see note 2, p. 47.

In vain do you worry,
my heart,
ignoring the possibilities
of your flesh and blood.

Wholly enchained
in animal intercourse,
how can you attain
the act of loving?

Plants may be sown
by the throwing of seeds,
but care is needed
for that joy of the eye:
the field heavy with golden rice.

౨ *Podo*

THE MIRROR OF THE SKY

That secret of feeling,
my heart,
is consciousness.
The riches wrapped
in a heap of rubbish
need discernment.
Sugar also glitters
when mingled with sand.

~ *Podo*[1]

I, a Collector in a broken-down village,
when the revenues came
the final accounts
revealed a deficit.
Even my own wealth was gone,
eaten away
by Time's devouring raids.

~ *Podo*

[1]Tape-recorded in Siuri, Birbhum, 1954. Singer: Nabanidās Bāul.

What makes you think
you are human?
Having squandered
your heart's heritage,
you are lost in lust.

It is senseless to scheme
with a lock and a key
against your fear
of your own weaknesses.
Your home is in a shambles
while the outhouse shines
below the moon's canopy.

God is deserting your temple
as you amuse yourself
by blowing conch shells
and ringing bells.

Podo[1]

[1]Tape-recorded in Siuri, Birbhum, in 1954. Singer: Nabanidās
Bāul.

You may hurt me, my lord,
go, hurt me
as long as I can bear the pain.

Sorrow weighs down on me
and I bear it, bending
in spite of my weakened limbs.

≈ Podo

A leper does not fret
over ordinary fever.
His bed being the ocean
he is not afraid of the dew.

When love is still true
to the anguish of parting,
sorrow for oneself
sinks in the sea of grief.

≈ Prasanna

Ants wishing to fly
are endowed with wings
but never can turn into birds.
They lose their lives
to devouring birds.

✍ Prasanna

Can the weak become weaker
wishing to be great?
You cannot be an ascetic
and yet long for fame.

Destroy the enemies of strength[1]
and raise the mirror
of wisdom in your hand.
To have the right to worship
you must straighten your crooked heart.

Learn reason from the soil of the land.

✍ Prasanna

[1]*Jnānendriya*: see note 1, p. 152.

The act of finding
is not for the highest.
By being humble
you can reach God.

Clouds pour rain
on the hollows of the earth
but the deepest wells
guard the water as a blessing.

❧ Prasanna

A rutting elephant repels control
but the keeper holds the beast
by his driving hook
and leads it to the battlefield.

Lust must be charged
with the arrow of love.
In the arena of passions,
the vigilant will never be vanquished.

❧ Prasanna

Prepare your heart
day by day
till it is ready
for the rise of the full moon.[1]
Then lay a trap
at the bottom of the river[2]
to catch it.

Pulin

Have you tallied,
my heart,
the number of ways
of finding him[3]
in the city of love?
The treasure of life
shuns bogus reckonings.

[1]*Chandra, chānd* and *Krishnachandra*—the moon and the black
moon—represent Krishna, God.
[2]River, symbol for life; boat, symbol for the human body.
[3]God, unattainable by the senses, formless.

The world is a carnival
where lovers meet
like children at play.
Understand
the nature of your feeling
for the jewel of your life.

He is reached in the way
each seeks to reach him:
through tender passion
or servitude,
through loyalty
or parental care,
or through the love
of tranquility, peace.

Find the feelings
which are born with you,
then worship him
with all your strength.

Punya

O my heart,[1]
imprisoned in a cave of darkness
forever ignorant,
you sleep unaware,
O my blind heart,
and the treasure of worship
slips away from you.

Why become drunk
on meaningless precepts?
What good is there in roaming
from place to place
never ceasing to think?
Instead of shaving your heart's desires
you have shaved your head
to look like a sage.

My foolish heart,
your passions like tigers
are ready to leap,
and the doors of the senses
are blocked by the mind.
How will you escape?
Purify the two poles of your being
and the Master will come to your aid.

Says Rādhānāth:
who can ferry you
across the stream of life
but God as your helmsman?
Abandon Master, my foolish heart,
and worship God.

~ Rādhānāth[2]

[1]*Mon*: see note 2, p. 47.
[2]Tape-recorded in Siuri, Birbhum, in 1954. Singer: Purna
Chandra, son of Nabanidās Bāul

194

Explore the nature
of your body,
my unfeeling heart.
Unless you know
your very substance,
worshipping God
is of no avail.
The body is the home
of seven heavens,
the nether-world
and the earth we live on[1]
for you to voyage in.
You will blunder
my unseeing heart,
as you never learnt to know
the friends and foes
alive in your body.

Rādhāshyām

---

[1]Heavens and nether world: see note 7, p. 73.

While desire
burns in the limbs
there is still time.
Boil the juice
on the fire of longing
to concentrate
the essence.

The sweetness of syrup
will ferment and sour
unless it is stirred
on controlled heat.
Feelings evolve from desire
and love shoots forth
from lust.

ϟ Rādhāshyām

That man[1] is living in man
wholly intermingled.
O my unseeing heart,
your eyes are unwise.
How then can you
find the treasured man?
The unseen man
dwelling in the brilliance of light
hides his identity
from those blinded by stupor.
He is stationed within
appearing and vanishing
as the eyelids blink.

         Rādhāshyām

---

[1]God, unattainable by the senses, formless.

Strange are the ways
of love
even when bound
by a beautiful form.
It may cause you tears,
laughter or smiles,
may make you dance or sing,
yet love washes away
the stains on fragile flesh.

⊷ Rājyeshwar

Now is the time for you
to repeat the names
of Rādhā and Krishna,
the gods of devoted love.

The central beam
of your life is down
and your time has gone.
Your cheeks are sunk
and your hair is slack,
dead as a mop of jute.
Now is the time to repeat
the names of Rādhā and Krishna.

A fading rainbow,
you balance on a stick,
bent as a letter of the alphabet,
knees and head together.
Your time has gone
and all for nothing.
Your teeth are missing
but your eyes,
through empty holes,
still frown from your brows.

Rāmachandra

My heart is eager enough
but shy at work.
It knows but never learns.
And as fast as an eyelid blinks
it creates catastrophes
and drives me from place to place.

My heart is like a horse
with five pairs of reins round its neck[1]
pulled in five directions at once
by five pairs of hands . . .

. . . My crippled heart
plays many tricks:
it talks of God
as it speaks of evil.

Rāma Gosāiñ
(Rāmachandra)

[1]The five elements: earth, water, fire, air, and ether.

Scholar!
What scriptures have you read
to back your pedantic pride?
You have yet to learn
the letters of the alphabet.

Rāmakrishna

Build a bridge
over the river
of life and death
to reach beyond.

Rāmalāl

The nectar of the moon
and the honey in the lotus,
how do they meet—
the moon from the sky
and the lotus from the lake?

Ramanadās

My plaited hair
is still intact and dry
though I stand in the stream
and splash and swim about the river.
I cannot be touched by water.

I tend to all the household work,
cooking, arranging, and offering food,
but I am not touched
by domestic life.

I am neither loyal nor disloyal,
but I cannot abandon my lord of love.[1]

Rasarāj Goswāmi[2]

[1]God, unattainable by the senses, formless.
[2]Tape-recorded in Siuri, Birbhum, in 1954. Singer: Purna
Chandra, son of Nabanidās Bāul.

My heart,
dress yourself
in the spirit of all women[1]
and reverse
your nature and habits.

Millions of suns
will burst open
with brilliance
and the formless
will be seen.

You will see
what cannot be seen
unless you become
the formless within you.

       ✍ *Rupchānd*

---

[1]*Prakriti* is a Sanskrit word meaning "matter," but to the average
Bāul it means feminine energy. In order to achieve full
consciousness, the Bāul considers that it is sometimes necessary
to adopt the opposite nature to one's own so as to be able to
unite the male and the female elements in oneself.

An urn of butter
balanced on his head,
the porter walked.
He dreamt of the cattle trade,
of money, marriage, and a son.
In his dream
his son came running
to call him home for food.
As the porter feigned anger
and refused to return,
the butter urn fell to pieces.

        ⊸ *Sudhir*

The senseless seldom gains wisdom,
as with my stupid heart
that puts out the lamp
in its own home
for fear of others.

        ⊸ *Tāran*

A creature of lust
is easily seen,
he is full of signs.
Like the ant
learning to fly
he is unafraid of death.
Like a vulture
soaring high
only to swoop
on a garbage heap,
a man of lust
falls for a bag of sex,
forgetting his vows.

Love never can be
found in lust alone.
Tāran,
worship your Master.

          ∾ *Tāran*

When swindlers hold a market
nature turns crooked
and heaven becomes merely a word.

          ∾ *Uttamā*

BIOGRAPHICAL NOTES

ৎ

Ananta

Well known among the West Bengal Bāuls, Ananta comes from Balshigram of Bankura district. He is said to have died toward the close of the nineteenth century.

Bishā Bhuñimāli

The song translated in this volume comes from the collection of Kshitimohan Sen Shastri. According to Mr. Sen Shastri, Bishā Bhuñimāli was a disciple of Balarām Bāul, who belonged to the Hindu Kaivarta caste.

Chandidās Gosāiñ

Chandidās Gosāiñ died in 1938, but his life is shrouded with many improbable stories, such as that he lived 151 years. He lived in Nabadwip but originally came from the *namashudra* caste from the village Kamarhati in the district of Jessore, now in Bangladesh. He left several disciples behind him.

Dwija Āshutosh

Hindu Bāul from West Bengal. The song by Āshutosh was collected from a Bāul singer in Betālban, district of Bardhaman. No other information available. Dates uncertain. *cf. Bānglār Bāul Gān*, Upendranath Bhattacharya, Calcutta, 1957.

Dwija Gadādhar

Hindu Bāul from West Bengal. Gadādhar's song was collected during an annual Bāul gathering at Kenduli, Birbhum. *cf. Bānglar Bāul O Bāul Gān.*

Erfan Shāh

Well-known Bāul from Barasat, district of 24 Parganas, West Bengal. Erfan Shāh has left a number of disciples behind him. Dates of birth and death are uncertain.

Gangārām

Gangārām belonged to the *namashudra* caste and, though older in age, was a great friend of Madan Bāul, also presented in this volume. The two songs translated here come from Kshitimohan Sen Shastri's collection. According to Mr. Sen Shastri's assessment, the teacher of Gangārām was Mādhā.

No precise date is available, but Gangārām, is known to have been a great Bāul.

Gaurchānd

Hindu Bāul from West Bengal. Gaurchānd's song was collected from a Bāul singer in Betālban, district of Bardhaman. No other information available. Dates uncertain. *cf. Bānglār Bāul O Bāul Gān.*

Gobinda Dās (possibly Godné Dās)

Hindu Bāul from West Bengal. Gobinda Dās's

songs were collected from a Bāul singer in Bétālban, in the district of Bardhaman. No other information available. Dates uncertain. *cf. Bānglār Bāul O Bāul Gān.*

Gosāiñ Gopāl, Gopāl (born Rāmgopāl Joyārdār)
Born in 1869, in the village of Shilaidaha, Kushtia, Rāmgopāl came from a Vaishnava Brahman family. Father: Rāmlāl Joyārdār. Mother: Manmohini. Guru: his father Rāmlāl.
Rāmgopāl learned to read and write at an early age but he was mainly interested in singing. He followed the Vaishnava faith as a Bāul, and had a large number of followers among both the Hindu and the Muslim communities. He was well known for his great healing powers. He changed his name into Gosāiñ Gopāl when he became a Bāul. Died June, 1912.

Hāudé Gosāiñ
Born of a brahman family in 1795, in Medtalā, Burdwan. His family name before becoming a Bāul was Matilāl Sānyāl. Father: Haladhar Sānyāl. Mother: Shyāmāsundari.
Well educated in Sanskrit literature and Hindu theology, Matilāl adopted the name of Hāudé Gosāiñ when he became a Bāul. He had two teachers: Bashishthānanda Swāmi, Matilāl's first teacher, who taught him the Tantrik texts, and Prahlādānanda Goswāmi, who was his teacher in Vaishnava theology

before Matilāl became a Bāul and adopted the name Hāudé.

Ishān Jugi (Ishān)

Ishān belonged to the Hindu Jugi caste, possibly related to the Nāth sect. He was the teacher of Madan Bāul, who came from an Islamic family. The songs of Ishān translated for this volume come from Kshitimohan Sen Shastri's collection. Dates uncertain, but judging from the language, Ishān's songs in their present Bengali version could not be older than the second half of the nineteenth century.

Jādubindu

Jādubindu came from the village of Panchloki in the district of Bardhaman. The dates of his birth and death are not known. His guru was a Bāul named Kubir.

Jādubindu has left a fairly large number of songs, probably a couple of hundred. A true Bāul, coming from the peasant background, Jādubindu uses the simple imagery of village life. The fisherman, the plowman, the boatman, and the tools of their respective trades are also the tools of Jādubindu's poetic work. As a result, his songs are extremely popular with the peasant communities of Bengal.

Jaladhar

Hindu Bāul from Bangladesh. Jaladhar's songs are known in the district of Dhaka. No other information available. Dates uncertain. *cf. Bānglār Bāul O Bāul Gān.*

Kālāchānd

Kālāchānd was a carpenter by profession and possibly belonged to the *namashudra* caste. His teacher was Nityanāth. Madan Bāul is said to have belonged to this tradition of Bāul teaching.

Lālan

Born in the village of Bhāndrā, previously in the district of Nadia, now in Kustia. His age is controversial, but it is estimated that he was born in 1775 B.C.E. and died in 1891. *cf. Bānglār Bāul O Bāul Gān.*

Lālan came from a Hindu Kāyastha family, the family name being Kar or Das. From childhood, he is known to have been oriented towards religion. According to the popular belief, Lālan was married young. During a walking pilgrimage to Puri, to the famous Hindu temple of Jagannāth, Lālan had a severe attack of smallpox and was abandoned by his travel companions for fear of contamination. A Muslim Bāul family took pity on him and brought him home. Lālan lived as a member of the family, joining the Bāul tradition, and eventually married a Muslim girl, his second wife.

Lālan's songs are as popular among the Bāuls of West Bengal as they are in the East, owing to his use of both Muslim and Hindu imagery and thought in his poems. Many of his songs were tape-recorded by the translator during his recording journey in West Bengal.

Madan

The majority of Madan Bāul's songs translated in this volume come from Kshitimohan Sen Shastri's collection. According to Mr. Sen Shastri, Madan was born a Mussulman. His guru was Ishān Jugi, belonging to the Hindu Jugi caste.

A great friend of Madan among the Bāuls was Gangārām, who is also presented in this book. Gangārām was older than Madan. Mr. Sen Shastri is cautious about dating Madan in his book *Bānglār Bāul* (University of Calcutta, 1954), but judging from the language these songs could not be older than late nineteenth century.

Miyājān Fakir

Muslim Bāul from Bangladesh. Songs of Miyājān Fakir are known in the Netrakona sub- division of the district of Dhaka. No other informa- tion available. Dates uncertain. *cf. Bānglār Bāul O Bāul Gān.*

Narahari Gosāin

Hindu Bāul from West Bengal. Narahari's songs were collected during an annual Bāul gathering at

Kenduli, Birbhum. *cf. Bānglār Bāul O Bāul Gān.*

Nitāidās

Hindu Bāul from West Bengal. No other information available. Dates uncertain.

Pānja Shāh

Born in the district of Jessore in 1851, Pānja Shāh died in 1914. Highly respected by the Bāuls of both Hindu and Muslim communities, his songs are fairly popular in different districts of Bengal, East and West.

Paramānanda

Hindu Bāul from West Bengal. No other information available. Dates uncertain.

Phatik Chānd (Gosāiñ Phatik)

Born in Faridpur, in a Hindu *namasudra* family, Phatik Chānd lived a long time in Nabadwip, the center of the Bengali Vaishnava movement. He died toward the middle of the twentieth century.

Podo (Padmalochan)

Very little information about Padmalochan's life is available, though it is commonly believed by the Bāuls of today that he came from the Rārh districts of Bengal and was an early Bāul whose songs have been passed orally from teacher to disciple. Some believe that Padmalochan may have lived toward the end of the eighteenth century. Some of his songs were known to Nabanidās Bāul of Siuri, Birbhum, whom I recorded in 1954.

Prasanna (Prasanna Kumār)
Hindu Bāul from West Bengal. No other information available. Dates uncertain.

Pulin
Hindu Bāul from Bangladesh. Pulin's songs are known in the district of Dhaka. No other information available. Dates uncertain. *cf. Bānglār Bāul O Bāul Gān.*

Rādhāshyām
Original home of Rādhāshyām (Dās) was in the village of Indas of district Bankura, but he lived mostly in Chandpur, Birbhum, in the ashram of his guru Guruchānd Goswāmi. Dates uncertain.

Rājyeshwar
Hindu Bāul from West Bengal. No other information available. Dates uncertain.

Rāmachandra (Rāma Gosāiñ)
Hindu Bāul from West Bengal. Rāmachandra's songs were collected from a Bāul singer in Betālban, district of Bardhaman. No other information available. Dates uncertain. *cf. Bānglār Bāul O Bāul Gān.*

Rāmakrishna

Hindu Bāul from West Bengal. No other information available. Dates uncertain.

Rāmalāl

Hindu Bāul from West Bengal. No other information available. Dates uncertain.

Ramanadās

Hindu Bāul from West Bengal. No other information available. Dates uncertain.

Sudhir

Hindu Bāul from West Bengal. The song by Sudhir was collected from a Bāul singer in Betālban, district of Bardhaman. No other information available. Dates uncertain. *cf. Bānglār Bāul O Bāul Gān.*

Tāran

Hindu Bāul from West Bengal. No other information available. Dates uncertain.

Uttamā

Hindu Bāul from West Bengal. Uttamā's song was collected from a Bāul singer in Betālban, district of Bardhaman. No other information available. Dates uncertain. *cf. Bānglār Bāul O Bāul Gān.*

BENGALI BIBLIOGRAPHY

ॐ

Bandopadhyay, A.K., *Paurāniki*, Vols. I & II, Calcutta, 1979.

Bandopadhyay, Somendranath, *Bānglār Bāul—Kāvya O Darshan*, Calcutta: University of Calcutta, 1964.

Bhattacharya, Ashutosh (ed.), *Bangiya Loka-Sangit Ratnākara*, Vol. I, Calcutta, 1966.

Bhattacharya, Upendranath, *Bānglār Bāul O Bāul Gān*, Calcutta, 1957.

Chakravarty, Amulyanath, *Bhārate Shakti Sādhānā*, Calcutta, Bengali year 1361.

Chattopadhyay, Pashupati (ed.), *Bāul Sangit*, Calcutta, 1964.

Das, Matilal and Piyushkanti Mahapatra (ed.), *Lālan Gitikā*, Calcutta, 1958.

Das, Tarachand (ed.), *Bāul Sangit*, Calcutta, 1961.

Deva, Chittaranjan, *Bānglār Palligiti*, Calcutta, 1966.

Devi, Indira, *Bānglār Sādhak Bāul*, Calcutta, 1962.

Hariharananda Bharati (transl.), *Mahānirvāna Tantra*, Calcutta, Bengali year 1320.

Ray, Kalidas, *Padāvali Sāhitya*, Calcutta, 1961.

_____ , *Prāchin Banga Sāhitya*, Vol. I, Calcutta, no date.

Ray, Sitanath (ed.), *Brihat Bāul Sangit*, Calcutta, no date.

Sen Shastri, Kshitimohan, *Bānglār Bāul*, Calcutta: University of Calcutta, 1954.

_____ , *Bānglār Sādhānā*, Calcutta, 1965.

_____ , *Hindu-Musalmāner Jukta Sādhanā*, Calcutta, 1949.

Shil, Nandalal (ed.), *Bāul Sangit*, Calcutta, no date.

ENGLISH BIBLIOGRAPHY

✧

Angarika Voginda Lama, *Art and Meditation*, Allahabad, 1936.

Archer, W.G., *The Loves of Krishna*, London, 1957.

Bagchi, Prabodh Chandra, *Studies in the Tantras*, Part One, Calcutta: University of Calcutta, 1939.

Ballantine, J.R. and Govind Shastri, *Yoga Sutras of Pātanjali*, Calcutta, 1955.

Basham, A.L., *The Wonder That Was India*, London, 1954.

Bhattacharya, Deben (transl.), *Love Songs of Vidyāpati*, London: W.G. Archer, 1963.

____ , *Love Songs of Chandidās*, London: 1967.

____ , *The Mirror of the Sky*, London: George Allen & Unwin, 1969.

____ , *Songs of Krishna*, New York: George Allen & Unwin, 1978.

Das Gupta, Sashi Bhusan, *An Introduction to Tantric*

Buddhism, Calcutta: University of Calcutta, 1950.

Dasgupta, Surendranath, *History of Indian Philosophy*, Five Vols., London, 1952–1955.

Eliade, Mircea, *Yoga, Immortality and Freedom*, London, 1958.

Mookerjee, Ajit, *Tantra Art*, Paris-New York-New Delhi, 1967.

_____ , *Tantra Asana*, Paris-New York-New Delhi, 1971.

Sen, Dinesh Chandra, *History of Bengali Language and Literature*, Calcutta, 1911.

Woodroffe, Sir John (Arthur Avalon), *Introduction to Tantra Shāstra*, Madras, 1952.

_____ , *The Serpent Power*, 12th ed., Madras, 1981.

DISCOGRAPHY

❧

BAM LD 099 *Religious Songs from Bengal—*
Songs of the Bāuls and Poems of Chandidās,
La Boite à   Musique, Paris.

BAM LD 015 Musique Religieuse de l'Inde,
La Boite à Musique, Paris.

V.41   Rhythmes et Melodies du   Bengale, Club
Français du   Disque, Paris.

CD: 92608 2 MUSIQUE DU MONDE—
BAULS BUDA Musique, Paris.

427 016 NE   Songs from Bengal, Philips,
Baarn, Holland.

SPL 1614   Folk Music of Northern India,
Period Records, New York.

ECLP 2256   Folk Songs of Bengal,
H.M.V., Dum Dum, India.

কে কথা কয়রে দেখা দেয় না।
নড়ে চড়ে হাতের কাছে,
খুঁজলে জনমভোর মেলে না।
কে কথা কয়রে দেখা দেয় না।
খুঁজি তারে আসমান জুড়ি,
আমারে চিনলে আমি,
এ সে বিষম ঘরের ঘরি,
আমি কোনজন সে কোন জনা।
কে কথা কয়রে দেখা দেয় না।

ঘরে বহিছে চলতে সেই জিন,
মিশিত জলে বায়ু হুতাশন,
শুকালে তার অন্বেষণ
মূর্শি বলে বেড়ে চলে না।
কে কথা কয়রে দেখা দেয় না।
হাতের আছে হয় না খবর,
ধনী দেখলে যাত দিল্লী লাহোর?
সিরাজ সাঁই কয় লালন রে
দেখ মনের ঘোর গেল না।
কে কথা কয়রে দেখা দেয় না।
হাতের আছে নড়ে চড়ে
খুঁজলে জনম ভোর মেলে না।
কে কথা কয়রে দেখা দেয় না॥

"Ké Kathā koyré"—Bāul Song by Lālan

APPENDIX A
NOTATION OF A SONG BY LĀLAN

ঔ

"Ké Kathā koyré"
Bāul Song by Lālan
Singer: Torap Shāh of Jessore, Bangladesh
Tape-recorded: Calcutta, 1971
Instrument: *Swarāj*, a lute of four melody strings
and five sympathetic strings.

KÉ KATHĀ KOYRÉ / DEKHĀ DEYNĀ
WHO TALKS / NOT SHOWING UP

KÉ KATHĀ KOYRÉ / DEKHĀ DEYNĀ
WHO TALKS / NOT SHOWING UP

NODÉ CHODÉ / HĀTÉR KĀCHNÉ
MOVES ABOUT / NEAR AT HAND

KHUÑJLÉ JANAMBHOR MÉLÉNĀ
WHEN SEARCHED / NOT TO BE FOUND IN WHOLE
LIFE

NODÉ CHODÉ / HĀTÉR KĀCHNÉ
MOVES ABOUT / NEAR AT HAND

THE MIRROR OF THE SKY

KHUÑJLÉ JANAMBHOR MÉLÉNĀ
WHEN SEARCHED / NOT TO BE FOUND IN WHOLE
   LIFE

KÉ KATHĀ KOYRÉ / DEKHĀ DEYNĀ
WHO TALKS / NOT SHOWING UP

KÉ KATHĀ KOYRÉ / DEKHĀ DEYNĀ
WHO TALKS / NOT SHOWING UP

KHUÑJI TĀRÉ / ĀSMĀN JOMI
I SEARCH FOR HIM / [IN THE] SKY [AND THE]
   EARTH

ĀMĀRÉ / CHINĪNÉ ĀMI
MYSELF / I DO NOT KNOW

KHUÑJI TĀRÉ / ĀSMĀN JOMI
I SEARCH FOR HIM / [IN THE] SKY [AND THE]
   EARTH

ĀMĀRÉ / CHINĪNÉ ĀMI
MYSELF / I DO NOT KNOW

É JÉ BISHOM / BHROMÉR BHROMI
THIS IS [A] GREAT / BLUNDERS' BLUNDERING IN

ĀMI KONJON / SÉ KONJONĀ
WHO AM I / WHO IS HE

É JÉ BISHOM / BHROMÉR BHROMI
THIS IS [A] GREAT / BLUNDERS' BLUNDERING IN

"Ké Kathā koyré"

ĀMI KONJON / SÉ KONJONĀ
WHO AM I / WHO IS HE

KÉ KATHĀ KOYRÉ / DEKHĀ DEYNĀ
WHO TALKS / NOT SHOWING UP

KÉ KATHĀ KOYRÉ / DEKHĀ DEYNĀ
WHO TALKS / NOT SHOWING UP

RĀM RAHIM / BOLTÉ SÉI JON
RĀM RAHIM / MEANS [THE] SAME PERSON

KSHITI JOL / BĀYU HUTĀSHON
SKY WATER / AIR FIRE

RĀM RAHIM / BOLTÉ SÉI JON
RĀM RAHIM / MEANS [THE] SAME PERSON

KSHITI JOL / BĀYU HUTĀSHON
SKY WATER / AIR FIRE

SHUDHĀLÉ / TĀR ONVÉSHON
ASKED / HIS WHEREABOUTS

MURKHA BOLÉ / KÉU BOLÉNĀ
FOOLS AS THEY ARE / NO ONE RESPONDS

SHUDHĀLÉ / TĀR ONVÉSHON
ASKED / HIS WHEREABOUTS

MURKHA BOLÉ / KÉU BOLÉNĀ
FOOLS AS THEY ARE / NO ONE RESPONDS

THE MIRROR OF THE SKY

KÉ KATHĀ KOYRÉ / DEKHĀ DEYNĀ
WHO TALKS / NOT SHOWING UP

KÉ KATHĀ KOYRÉ / DEKHĀ DEYNĀ
WHO TALKS / NOT SHOWING UP

HĀTÉR KĀCHNÉ / HOY NĀ KHABAR
NEAR AT HAND / [YOU] HAVE NO INFORMATION

KI DÉKHTÉ / JĀO DILLI LĀHOR
TO SEE WHAT / DO YOU GO TO DEHLI [AND]
    LAHORE

HĀTÉR KĀCHNÉ / HOY NĀ KHABAR
NEAR AT HAND / [YOU] HAVE NO INFORMATION

KI DÉKHTÉ / JĀO DILLI LĀHOR
TO SEE WHAT / DO YOU GO TO DEHLI [AND]
    LAHORE

SIRĀJ SHĀ / KOY LĀLON RE
SIRĀJ SHĀH SAYS OH LĀLAN

DÉKHÉ MONÉR / GHOR GELONĀ
HAVING SEEN / MIND'S STUPOR PERSISTS

SIRĀJ SHĀ / KOY LĀLON RE
SIRĀJ SHĀH SAYS OH LĀLAN

DÉKHÉ MONÉR / GHOR GELONĀ
HAVING SEEN / MIND'S STUPOR PERSISTS

"Ké Kathā koyré"

KÉ KATHĀ KOYRÉ / DEKHĀ DEYNĀ
WHO TALKS / NOT SHOWING UP

KÉ KATHĀ KOYRÉ / DEKHĀ DEYNĀ
WHO TALKS / NOT SHOWING UP

HĀTHÉR KĀCHNÉ / NODÉ CHODÉ
NEAR AT HAND / MOVES ABOUT

KHUÑJLÉ JANAMBHOR MÉLÉNĀ
WHEN SEARCHED / NOT TO BE FOUND IN WHOLE
LIFE.

HĀTHÉR KĀCHNÉ / NODÉ CHODÉ
NEAR AT HAND / MOVES ABOUT

KHUÑJLÉ JANAMBHOR MÉLÉNĀ
WHEN SEARCHED / NOT TO BE FOUND IN WHOLE
LIFE.

KÉ KATHĀ KOYRÉ / DEKHĀ DEYNĀ
WHO TALKS / NOT SHOWING UP

KÉ KATHĀ KOYRÉ / DEKHĀ DEYNĀ
WHO TALKS / NOT SHOWING UP

KÉ KATHĀ KOYRÉ / DEKHĀ DEYNĀ
WHO TALKS / NOT SHOWING UP

225

Ké Kathā Koyré

Bāul Song by Lālan

Singer: Torap Shāh of Jessore, Bangladesh
Tape-recorded: Calcutta, 1971
Notation: Danica Radman

No - dé cho - dé hā- té - r kā - chhé khu-ñj lé ja - nam

bho-r mé lé - nā

The Mirror of the Sky

"Ké Kathā koyré"

The Mirror of the Sky

APPENDIX B
SONG LYRICS FOR THE ACCOMPANYING CD
∾

1. ORE ĀMĀR ABODH MON

Attributed to Radhanath, addressing, possibly, a disciple
named Krishnadas, 19th century.

> O my senseless heart, you are forever unconscious.
> Asleep, you have squandered the treasures of life,
>   unaware.
> The three requirements of life[1] have gone berserk.
> What is the point of your roaming—like a monk—
>   with a shaved head but without a clean heart?
> Eager to pounce are the six tigers[2]
> through the nine vents of your body[3].
> Go and clean yourself from top to bottom
> for only then your Master will appear in your vision.
> Gosāin Radhanath says: How will you cross the river
>   of life, O Krishnadas, without your guru ferrying
>   you?
> And yet, my heart, my insane heart,
> leaving the guru aside you must worship God
>   (Govinda).

Sung by Purnadas when he was about nineteen years
old during an open-air public performance, together with
his father, Nabanidas Bāul. As he sang, Purnadas danced
with ankle-bells tied around his ankles, while accom-
panying himself on the plucking-drum, *ānandalahari*. He
was assisted by Sudhananda, who provided the instrumental
accompaniment on the long-necked lute, *dotārā*. All three

of them came from Siuri, Birbhum (West Bengal).
Recorded by courtesy of Banga Samskriti Sammelan,
Calcutta, 1954. Duration: 8.05 minutes.

Notes:
[1]*Triguna:* three primal qualities—virtues, vices, and the
ability to act.
[2]*Shadripu:* six inherent vices or enemies—sexual desire,
anger, greed, infatuation, vanity, and envy.
[3]*Navadwār:* the nine doors or openings of the body—eyes,
ears, nose, mouth, anus, and the genital.

2. *GAUR CHĀNDER HĀSPĀTĀLE*
Attributed to Ananta Bāul, 19th century.

> Brother, why should we endure any more pain?
> We have suffered enough.
> Come, all of you who wish to visit the hospital of
> Gaurchand[1] in the city of Nadia.
> Never have we seen such relief from sufferings
> exploring the city's clinics day after day.
> Come, all of you who wish to visit the hospital of
> Gaurchand in the city of Nadia.
>
> God is the absolute chief of the hospital.
> Nityananda[2] and Shrinibas[3] are there too,
> with Haridas[3], the compounder, mixing the medicine.
> They have painted a sign three stories high
> and have in store what you cannot find today.
> The patients are rolling in with one leading the other.
>
> Nityananda has a great reputation
> having patients such as Jagai and Madhai—notorious
> bandits of the time—who were cured in no time.

Come, all of you who wish to visit the hospital of
Gaurchand.

God has created the medicinal plants
but the medicine is made from a formula with care and
the diet is prescribed by the physician.
Finally, they all dissolve in the devotion to God.

Gosāin, the wise one, suggests in his turn,
you will get cured, O senseless one, and conquer your
illness.
Come, all of you who wish to visit the hospital of my
Gaurchand.

This is an allegorical song in which mater- ialism is
treated as an illness. Presented by the group from Siuri
mentioned in the previous song, it was sung by Nabanidas
Bāul, who accompanied himself on the *ānandalahari* as he
danced wearing *ghunghur* on his ankles. Toward the middle
of the song, Purnadas joins his father in singing for a short
while and then withdraws. *Dotārā* by Sud- hananda.
Recorded by courtesy of Banga Samskriti Sammelan,
Calcutta, 1954. Duration: 8.00 minutes.

Notes:
[1]Gaurchand—the clear Moon—refers lovingly to Shri
Gauranga or Shri Chaitanya Deva, the 16th century
Vaishnava (devotee of Vishnu) teacher from Nabadwip, or
Nadia, West Bengal, as he was a fair-skinned man.
[2]Nityananda, chief religious associate of Shri Chaitanya
Deva.
[3]Other associates of Shri Chaitanya Deva.

233

THE MIRROR OF THE SKY

3. *MONRE ĀMĀR ĀPAN KHABAR*
Attributed to Lalan, c. 1775-1891.

O my heart, I have no knowledge of my self.
If for once I could know what I am,
the unknown would be known.

God is near and yet far away,
like the mountain hiding behind the hair hanging in my
    eyes.
I travel to the distant towns of Dhaka and Delhi,
constantly searching.
But I am only circling around my knees.

God is alive in my living room.
Only purity of heart will lead me to him.
The more I study the wisdom of the Vedas[1],
    the more I am bewildered repeating "I."
O my heart, seek shelter at the feet of he who knows
    the word "I."

Lalan says with a confused heart:
I am blind in spite of my eyes.

Song and instruments by Bhaktadas Baul and Group.
Instruments: *sārindā* (bowed instrument of folk origin) and
the kettle-drum, *duggi*. Recorded in Calcutta in February,
1954. Duration: 3.20 minutes.

Note:
[1]The Vedas constitute the earliest available sacred texts of
India. Four in number, they are *Rigveda, Yajurveda,
Sāmaveda,* and *Atharvaveda.* While the first three are
available in their entirety, *Athar- vaveda* exists only in
fragments and quotations. The assessed dates of the Vedas
vary widely, from 3000 B.C.E. to 1500 B.C.E.

234

4. TĀJMAHALE DOL LEGECHHE

Anonymous

The rites of spring have burst in the Tāj Mahal.
The meaning of the words
right and wrong, life and death,
are cast away into the empty space of meaninglessness.

The rites of spring have burst in the Tāj Mahal.
Little sons of pigs who were ruled by the powerful
    king
have gone out of control, taking charge of all.

The rites of spring have burst in the Tāj Mahal.
The owner of the land living in Mulādhār[1]
with zero income and expenses high
is unable to tally the accounts
while death surveys the treasury.

Song and instrumental accompaniment by Rama- krishna
Bāul Sangha, Howrah (West Bengal). Instruments: *aektārā,*
ānandalahari, bānshi, mandirā, violin, and the *tablā.*
Recorded February, 1954. Duration: 6.20 minutes.

Note:
[1]*Mulādhār* meant "root-base" in the Yogic concept of
Shatchakra, (the six lotus circles in the subtle body), and is
a four-petalled lotus. It is placed at the root of the spine
near the anal region. The other *Chakras* rising upward are:
Svādhishthāna of six petals situated at the root of the
genitals; centered on the naval is *Manipuraka* of ten petals;
the Heart Lotus *Anāhata* is of twelve petals; at the base of
the throat is the *Vishuddha* with sixteen petals; and between
the brows is *Ājnā* of two petals, which is regarded as the
seat of Brahman, the cosmic consciousness, energized by
the sonic symbol *Aum.*

5. *JADI CHARBI EROPLENE*
Anonymous

> If you wish to board an airplane, you must travel light
>   to be safe from the danger of a crash.
> You must renounce your errors and inhibitions
> and show your credentials at the airport.
> Paying your fare of devotion to God
> you must give up your worldly wealth to buy a ticket
>   for a seat.
> The feet of your guru, the airplane,
> will carry you to Vishnu's sphere[1] in less than an
>   eyelid's wink.
> Nityananda[2] is flying the aircraft, night and day,
>   floating on the air, like one who knows the five
>   vital airs of the body.[3]
> You have to be cautious and faithful to your guru.
> The ways of the airline are crooked
> but the aircraft is flown with loving care and trust in
>   the teacher, leading to Shri Chaitanya.[4]

Sung by a wandering Bāul, Haripada Debnath, a refugee
from East Pakistan, which is now Bangladesh. Haripada
Debnath accompanied himself on the *dotārā* that he made
with his own hands. Recorded in Varanasi in 1954.
Duration: 4.35 minutes.

Notes:
[1]Vishnu is the preserving power of the Hindu triple forces,
the other two being Brahma, creation, and Shiva,
dissolution. Vishnu's sphere in heaven is known as
Vaikuntha. In Bengali, as in this song, it is called Golok.
[2]Nityananda—cf. note 2, song No. 2.
[3]*Panchavayu*—the five vital airs, or breaths, called *prāna*,
apāna, *samāna*, *udāna* and *vyāna*, that are inhaled or
exhaled out of the body.
[4]Shri Chaitanya—cf. note 1, song No.2.

Songs of the Bāuls of Bengal—CD Lyrics

6. KE KATHĀ KAYRE
Lalan, c. 1775-1891

> Who is it that talks to me but does not let me see him?
> He moves close to my hands but away from my reach
>   in spite of my lifetime's search.
> I explore the sky and the earth searching for him,
> circling round my error of not knowing myself.
> Who am I and who is he?
>
> He is both, Rama and Rahim,
> He is earth, water, air and fire.
> Fools cannot lead you to Him in your search for Him.
> If you are unable to reach what is close to your hands,
>   what can you find in [distant] Delhi and Lahore?
> Siraj Shah says, O Lalan,
> the more I see the more I am confused.

Song and instrumental accompaniment on the *swarāj* (also a lute, like the *dotārā*, but with five sympathetic strings), by Torap Ali Shah, a Sufi Bāul from Jessore, East Pakistan, now Bangladesh, and with *ghunghur* and *kāthkartāl* (wooden clappers). It was recorded in 1971 in Calcutta when Torap Ali Shah came to India as a refugee during the Bangladesh war with Pakistan. Duration: 4.05 minutes.

237

7. HĀOYĀR GĀCHHE PHAL DHARECHHE
Attributed to Lalan, c.1775–1891.

Come, if you wish to see how fruits grow in a tree of
air.
O my heart, with leaves of air, vines of air, the tree of
air talks.
A circle of air in a human river, spins out sound,
creating air.
What an achievement of the master craftsman to bring
forth a single fruit on two separate trees.
Each month the tidal waves cause the fruit to grow.

That fruit, afloat on yoga, was achieved by worship
and prayer.
Lalan, hoping to have the fruit, says it is not meant for
me.

This is an allegorical song comparing men and women with
trees that breathe, and the monthly high tide with the
period of fertility. Sung with instrumental accompaniment
on the *swarāj* by the Bāul Torap Ali Shah of Jessore,
Bangladesh. Recorded in Calcutta, 1971. Duration: 4.05
minutes.

8. SWARĀJ, INSTRUMENTAL MUSIC
It is played by the Bāul Torap Ali Shah of Jessore,
Bangladesh. The *swarāj* is a long-necked lute with
skin-covered belly, like the *dotārā*, and is played with a
buffalo-horn plectrum. It has four melody strings and five
sympathetic strings. Re- corded in Calcutta, 1971.
Duration:1.30 minutes.

Songs of the Bāuls of Bengal—CD Lyrics

9. (A) ĀMĀR NEI KONO SAMBAL
Anonymous, sung by Dilip Bāul.

9. (B) DUI MON HOLE PARBI PHERE
Anonymous, sung by Hemanta Bāul.

Accompanied by *aektārā, dotārā, bānshi* (transverse bamboo flute), *ānandalahari* and cymbals, these two songs were recorded during a gathering of the Bāul musicians at the annual Bāul fair in Kenduli, Birbhum (West Bengal), in 1973. Every year during the winter solstice—as usual in the month of January—Bāuls from all over Bengal gather in this small West Bengal village, Kenduli, to pay their homage to the great 12th century Sanskrit songwriter Jayadeva, who used to live here. Here are the words of the two songs in translation:

(A) With no resources of my own
or any strength of faith,
my total need requires you ferry me
over the river of life.

The boat casts off while I stand
crying on the bank.
If you smile, beneficent God,
your feet will carry me across.

Duration: 7.00 minutes

(B) You must be single-minded
to visit the court of my Gaurchand.[1]
If your mind is torn in two
you will swim in a quandary`
and never reach the shore.

The court has ordered the queen of love,
Radha, to ferry all across,
but only after the mind is measured.
The jewelers who weigh are strict
and the scales accurate.
A wood-cutter is no judge
of precious stones;
the ox that carries the sweet-maker's load
knows no taste of sugar.
Gold is known to the goldsmith
who knows the art of testing it.

Duration: 5.45 minutes

Note:
[1]Gaurchand—cf. note 1, Song No. 2

10. ĀMĀR ATI SUNDAR EI RANGMAHALE

Rats are eating at my beautiful bejeweled home.
Rats have invaded my clay hut.
The divine craftsman had built the bejeweled home set
    with red rubies and precious stones.
Red rubies, my heart,
and with a heap of silk piled over the royal tower.

While I was absorbed with the glittering world, rats
    had sneaked into my room.
Now they are bouncing all over the place, eating the
    rice paddy and leaving only the husk.
Rats have invaded my clay hut.

Songs of the Bāuls of Bengal—CD Lyrics

Light the lamp of knowledge in your hut
to prevent the rats from destroying rice.
Expert in stealing, they enter after surveying the place.
There are six rats[1] in the room to empty the store of
rice but the cat of wisdom could catch them.
The wise ones will seek out and set the trap for the
rats.
My clay hut is invaded by rats.

Set to traditional melody, the words are written and
sung by Muhammad Hares Sardar, President, Bāul Shilpi
Samiti, Dhaka, Bangladesh. Accom- panied by the *dotārā*,
bamboo flute, harmonium and a barrel drum called the
dhol. Recorded in Dhaka in August, 1997. Duration: 6.00
minutes.

Note:
[1]The "six rats" refer to *Shad-ripu*, the six cardinal vices or
enemies of man, namely, sexual desire, anger, greed,
infatuation, vanity, and envy.

As evident from the text, these songs were recorded
during the years of 1954, 1971, 1973 and 1979. They
represent songs of the Bāuls from both of the Bengals:
West Bengal in India and today's Bangladesh, known as
East Bengal before the partition of India in 1947 and then
East Pakistan when the country became the eastern wing of
Pakistan. East Pakistan was named Bangladesh after the
war of independence with Pakistan in 1971.

INDEX

245

ABOUT THE AUTHOR

～

Deben Bhattacharya is a specialist in collecting, filming and recording traditional music, song and dance in Asia, Europe and North Africa. Since 1955 he has been producing documentary films, records, illustrated books and radio programs related to his research.

His films for TV and programs for radio on traditional music and rural life have been broadcast by the BBC, Thames Television, Channel Four, London; WDR Music TV, Cologne; Sveriges Radio/TV, Stockholm; BRT-3, Brussels; Door-darshan-TV, Calcutta; English TV, Singapore; POLTEL, Warsaw; Korean Television, Seoul, and others.

— MUSIC —

Mr. Bhattacharya has produced more than 130 LP albums of traditional music recorded in thirty-eight countries of Asia and Europe. These albums have been released by Philips, Baarn, Holland; ARGO (Decca Group); HMV and Columbia, London; Angel Records and Westminster, New York; OCORA, Disque BAM, Contrepoint, Paris; Supraphone, Prague; HMV, Calcutta; Nippon-Westminster and King Records, Tokyo; 25 LPs of Decca-ARGO Ethnic series have just been re-issued on CD by Polygram-Japan.

Currently he is producing three CD series that are being released by Vista-International, Edison, USA and Fremeaux and Associates, Paris; New Earth Record, Munich, and ARC Music Productions, USA and UK.

— BOOKS —

Deben Bhattacharya is the author of numerous books of translations of Indian medieval poetry and songs, including *Love Songs of Chandidas, Songs of Krishna* and *Love Songs of Vidyapati. The Mirror of the Sky* was first published by George Allen & Unwin Ltd., London, 1969, for the UNESCO Collection of Representative Works, Indian Series and as *Songs of the Bards of Bengal,* Grove Press, New York, 1969.

He has also published three books of photographs with EP and LP records—*The Gypsies* (London, 1965); *La Semaine Sainte en Andalousie* (Paris, 1960); *Visage d'Israel* (Paris, 1960).

— FILM —

"Asian Insights"which is a series of twenty-two documentary films on the performing arts of Asia covering Turkey, India, China, Taiwan, Thailand, Bali, Sri Lanka, Nepal and the Indian side of the Himalayas for the Tibetan films call "Echoes from Tibet," and "The Chanting Lama" has been shown by major TV stations in Europe and Asia, as listed above. This series also includes "Music from Hungary" and "Music in Rumania."

ADDITIONAL TITLES FROM HOHM PRESS

RENDING THE VEIL: Literal and Poetic Translations of Rumi
by Shahram T. Shiva
Preface by Peter Lamborn Wilson

With a groundbreaking transliteration, English-speaking lovers of Rumi's poetry will have the opportunity to "read" his verse aloud, observing the rhythm, the repetition, and the rhyme that Rumi himself used over 800 years ago. Offers the reader a hand at the magical art of translation, providing a unique "word by word" literal translation from which to compose one's own variations. Together with exquisitely-rendered Persian calligraphy of 252 of Rumi's quatrains (many previously untranslated), Mr. Shiva presents his own poetic English version of each piece. From his study of more than 2000 of Rumi's short poems, the translator presents a faithful cross-section of the poet's many moods, from fierce passion to silent adoration.

"Faithfully polished translations." – *Publisher's Weekly*

Cloth, 280 pages, $27.95, ISBN: 0-93425246-7

• • •

FOR LOVE OF THE DARK ONE: SONGS OF MIRABAI
Revised edition
Translations and Introduction by Andrew Schelling

Mirabai is probably the best known poet in India today, even though she lived 400 years ago (1498-1593). Her poems are ecstatic declarations of surrender to and praise of Krishna, whom she lovingly calls "The Dark One." Mira's poetry is as alive today as it was in the sixteenth century—a poetry of freedom, of breaking with traditional stereotypes, of trusting completely in the benediction of God. It is also some of the most exalted mystical poetry in all of world literature, expressing her complete surrender to the Divine, her longing, and her madness in love. This revised edition contains the original 80 poems, a completely revised Introduction, updated glossary, bibliography and discography, and additional Sanskrit notations.

Paper, 128 pages, $12.00, ISBN: 0-934252-84-X

TO ORDER, PLEASE SEE ACCOMPANYING ORDER FORM.

ADDITIONAL TITLES FROM HOHM PRESS

CRAZY AS WE ARE

Selected Rubais from the Divan-i-Kebir of Mevlana Celaleddin Rumi

Introduction and Translation by Dr. Nevit O. Ergin

This book is a collection of 128 previously untranslated *rubais*, or quatrains (four-line poems which express one complete idea), of the 13th-century scholar and mystic poet Rumi. Filled with the passion of both ecstasy and pain, Rumi's words may stir remembrance and longing, or challenge complacency in the presence of awesome love. Ergin's translations (directly from Farsi, the language in which Rumi wrote) are fresh and highly sensitive, reflecting his own resonance with the path of annihilation in the Divine as taught by the great Sufi masters.

Paper, 88 pages, $9.00, ISBN 0-934252-30-0

• • •

THE YOGA TRADITION: Its History, Literature, Philosophy and Practice

by Georg Feuerstein, Ph.D.

Foreword by Ken Wilber

A complete overview of the great Yogic traditions of: Raja-Yoga, Hatha-Yoga, Jnana-Yoga, Bhakti-Yoga, Karma-Yoga, Tantra-Yoga, Kundalini-Yoga, Mantra-Yoga and many other lesser known forms. Includes translations of over twenty famous Yoga treatises, like the *Yoga-Sutra* of Patanjali, and a first-time translation of the *Goraksha Paddhati*, an ancient Hatha Yoga text. Covers all aspects of Hindu, Buddhist, Jaina and Sikh Yoga. A necessary resource for all students and scholars of Yoga.

"Without a doubt the finest overall explanation of Yoga. Destined to become a classic." – Ken Wilber

Paper, 708 pages, Over 200 illustrations, $39.95, ISBN: 0-934252-83-1.
Cloth, $49.95, ISBN: 0-934252-88-2

• • •

CROSSING THE RIVER OF LOVE: Music of the Bauls of Bengal

A live recording of Sanatan Das Baul and sons during their tour of Western U.S., Spring 1991. Audiences from San Diego to Seattle delight in the Baul's passionate brand of song and dance.

1 audio-cassette, 90 minutes, $11.95, 0-934252-38-6

TO ORDER, PLEASE SEE ACCOMPANYING ORDER FORM.

RETAIL ORDER FORM FOR HOHM PRESS BOOKS

ame _____ Phone (   ) _____

reet Address or P.O. Box _____

ty _____ State _____ Zip Code _____

QTY	TITLE	ITEM PRICE	TOTAL PRICE	
	RENDING THE VEIL	$27.95		
	FOR LOVE OF THE DARK ONE	$12.00		
	CRAZY AS WE ARE	$9.00		
	THE YOGA TRADITION, CLOTH	$49.95		
	THE YOGA TRADITION, PAPER	$39.95		
	CROSSING THE RIVER OF LOVE	$11.95		
	MIRROR OF THE SKY (BOOK & CD)	$24.95		
	MIRROR OF THE SKY - CD ONLY	$14.95		
		SUBTOTAL:		
		SHIPPING: (see below)		
		TOTAL:		

RFACE SHIPPING CHARGES

book $4.00

h additional item $1.00

IP MY ORDER

Surface U.S. Mail—Priority 2nd-Day Air (Mail + $5.00)

☐ UPS (Mail + $2.00)
☐ Next-Day Air (Mail + $15.00)

THOD OF PAYMENT:

Check or M.O.   Payable to Hohm Press, P.O. Box 2501, Prescott, AZ 86302

Call 1-800-381-2700 to place your credit card order

Or call 1-520-717-1779 to fax your credit card order

Information for Visa/MasterCard order only:

_____ – _____ – _____ – _____   Expiration Date _____

Visit our Website to view our complete catalog: www.hohmpress.com

ORDER NOW! Call 1-800-381-2700 or fax your order to 1-520-717-1779.
(Remember to include your credit card information.)